True GOD

A Guide to Recognizing and Building a Relationship with God

F. M. Pal

Independently Published

ISBN 978-1-972377-00-0

To

My Parents

Visit the author's website:

fmpal.net

Table of Contents

Acknowledgements

Belief is shaped by the values we hold and the experiences we live. I am deeply grateful to my parents, whose steadfast commitment to their beliefs provided me with a healthy and stable foundation. Their lives were a testament to the beliefs they held, and the experiences they provided me profoundly influenced the path I have taken. Without them, this book would not have been possible.

Introduction

The concept of God is foundational to life since it offers an explanation for the fundamental questions about life: Where did we come from? Why are we here? Where are we going? Therefore, it is important to understand and accurately define this concept. And considering the importance of the subject matter and the track record of human civilization, perhaps no other concept in the history of humankind has been so misrepresented as the concept of God. For some, God is a fantastical, mythical being that must be accepted with blind and unquestionable faith. For others, it is an entity that must be explained and grasped like some physical object in order to find acceptance. How is it possible for this same God to have such wildly different interpretations?

As a result of these contradictions, many have decided to forego the idea of God altogether. One argument put forth by such atheists is that if there is indeed a God, then there should be a universally accepted understanding of God that appeals to the minds and hearts of all human beings. And humanity's disagreement on a universally accepted concept points to the non-existence of God. In short, the misrepresentations and misconceptions about God that we as human beings have created over time have, sadly enough, contributed to the denial of the existence of God altogether[1].

---

[1] The importance of attaining the correct recognition of God cannot be overstated. It is the first step in the process to building a relationship

So the natural question that arises is: can we arrive at the true, universally accepted concept of God that appeals to both the mind and the heart? And subsequently, how can we establish a relationship with this God to then transform this concept into reality for us? This book attempts to answer these two fundamental questions.

But before proceeding any further, let's address the preliminary question: Why should one even bother to take the time and seek answers to these questions? It is important to address this adequately so that the reader can be sufficiently convinced that this journey is worth taking.

One answer is hinted at in the very title of the book. What we aim to do is seek the truth about God. Truth has an intrinsic value that falsehood simply does not and as thinking human beings, we are naturally inclined towards seeking the truth. Generally speaking, the significance of arriving at the truth of something is proportional to the importance of that thing. Now putting aside, for a moment, one's belief or lack thereof in God, one can argue that there is nothing greater in importance than the concept of God because it lies at the root of our most fundamental existential questions. So we can logically conclude that if there is anything in the world worth spending time on, it is indeed the pursuit of arriving at the truth about the concept of God.

---

with the Creator and if wrongly taken, can lead one astray. For example, if a person sets up an animal, or any of the elements—such as fire, water, sun—or even a human being as their god, it cannot be expected that their subsequent steps taken along that path would lead to success. Atheism is an extreme case response to this phenomenon where an individual decides to completely forgo their belief in a Higher Being due to erroneous concepts.

Another answer to this question can be given by taking a holistic look at what it means to be human—what constitutes the full human experience. If we can show that the recognition of God leads to a more complete human experience, then it is undoubtedly worthwhile to spend our time and effort pursuing it.

As humans, we naturally gravitate toward a fulfilling and complete life rather than one that is lacking or diminished. And the totality of human existence, the components that make up the full human experience, are best described using the mind-body-soul triad. Across philosophy, religion, and psychology, thinkers have repeatedly divided the human experience into physical, mental, and spiritual (or inner) dimensions. The mind-body-soul triad is one of the most enduring expressions of this pattern. So a full human experience is naturally one that would cater to all three components of this triad[2].

---

[2] For anyone who may deny the existence of the soul altogether, it is worth spending some time to clarify this subject. When it comes to the body, it is very easy to acknowledge its existence. We use the basic senses of sight, taste, touch etc. to conclude that the body in its physical form does indeed exist. When it comes to mind, even though the concept is a bit more subtle in that we can't use the basic senses to acknowledge the existence of the mind, we can readily agree that the phenomenon of knowledge, understanding, and intellect does exist and we attribute it to this thing called the mind. (Note that we define the mind as something different from the physical mass known as the brain and we can all agree that the sublime concept of the mind finds a home in the physical entity of the brain.) Now it is easy to note that the totality of our existence is not limited to the body and the mind—there is more to it. For example, human beings have emotions—something that we cannot ascribe to the body nor the mind. We also feel love, a phenomenon that cannot be described purely on a physical or intellectual basis. In other words, the totality of human existence goes

When we analyze our pursuit towards living the full human experience, we come to the realization that we spend a good portion of our lives focusing on sharpening our mind through formal and informal education. Likewise, we try to take care of our bodies—sometimes paying excessive amounts of money for diet or exercise programs—and in cases where our body may fall victim to sickness or injury, we go to great lengths to find a cure. But when it comes to our soul, we are neglectful, not spending even a fraction of the effort on the needs of our soul. And those who at least realize the need to take care of the soul often resort to ineffective or incorrect means, not necessarily due to any fault of their own but rather due to lack of knowledge or understanding. Given that the totality of human existence does indeed consist of the three components stated above, then common sense dictates that all three components must be cared for in order to live the complete human experience and neglecting any one component would lead to a relatively incomplete life. So what we aim to do through this book is to cater to this neglected component of the complete human experience. *In more practical terms, the value proposition is that by following the process outlined herein, one should be able to, at a minimum, bring into balance the neglected component of the mind-body-soul triad, which in turn should equip one to handle the challenges of life much more effectively, eventually leading to the satisfaction of having lived a more complete and fulfilled life when it comes time to face death*[3]*.*

---

beyond the body and the mind, and in the most basic terms, the remaining part can be ascribed to the soul.

[3] This last point is important: death is the ultimate reality check on life. If there is one instance when, as the expression goes, your whole life passes in front of you, it is at the time of death. No one has ever come back to life after having died. (All the stories about near-death

A third answer to why we should take the time and effort to undertake this journey can be obtained by studying the individual and collective social constructs that humanity has created to improve life. Such an analysis can help us understand the direct, practical benefits that belief in God can provide in aiding these social constructs and improving our daily lives.

We will illustrate this point through the example of the fundamental social construct of crime and punishment. An argument can be made that crime—be it personal, domestic, or societal—is rooted in the idea of lack of accountability. It is a well-established fact that the likelihood of committing a crime is significantly reduced if an individual knows that he or she will be held accountable. For an atheist, this accountability comes at the hand of human authority—be it a parent for a child, a policeman for a citizen, or a government for a nation etc. However, these authorities are fundamentally limited—their knowledge is limited, their visibility is limited, their scope is limited. But when it comes to a believer, the authority is God, Who is All-Powerful, All-Seeing,

---

experiences always involve "partial death.") Whether one believes in the afterlife or not (a topic we will cover later in the book), it is certain that death is the final gateway from which there is no return. And it behooves us to be prepared for death. No matter how successful one may be in life, when on the death bed, most are left anxious. The problem is that no one comes back from that state to have the advantage of hindsight. And most are not bothered enough to anticipate it and prepare for it. There are many stories of men and women who, according to the worldly definition, achieved greatness in life but when they lay on their deathbed, felt great regret and sorrow for not having catered to the needs of the soul, needs which if addressed throughout one's life would have resulted in reducing the restlessness at the time of death, needs which center around the idea of True God.

All-Encompassing. We should ask ourselves the hypothetical question: if we know for certain that there is a supreme God Who is not only watching everything we do but also knows everything our mind is thinking and everything our heart is feeling, and further, has certain expectations of us to do good and avoid evil, would we not try and live a life according to those expectations? Doing good and avoiding evil then becomes a deep-rooted practice that emanates from a profound awareness of accountability to a Higher Being. It no longer remains a cat-and-mouse game of hiding from worldly authorities to commit crimes in secrecy because there is no secret that is hidden from God. With this understanding, a true and firm belief in God leads to a better, more peaceful world. (This is not to say that man-made social constructs such as policing and prisons are not necessary. Rather they become much more effective if built on the foundation that God is Omnipotent, Omniscient, and Omnipresent.)

We glossed over the idea of personal crime in our discussion above, but it warrants a deeper analysis because it lies at the root of all other types of crimes and again, is impacted by one's belief in God. When we speak of personal crime, we mean crime committed against oneself. It can also be equated to the concept of committing sin. For example, when someone decides to hurt another person, it first takes root in his/her heart. It may be jealousy, revenge, arrogance or a number of other similar emotions that cause a feeling of ill will towards the other person which then translates into ill action. If that person were to have true belief in a God that despises jealousy, discourages revenge, and forbids arrogance, then he/she would not be as likely to foster such feelings in the heart, which would then curtail any potential ill action at its root. All this to say that any crime or offense first takes root in the heart (in the form of personal crime or sin), which then leads to devising a scheme in the mind, which then translates to some physical ill action committed by the body. And if a person is convinced that there is an All-Knowing God who dislikes sin, he/she is less likely to commit a crime. Defined in this light, *all social crime fundamentally has its origin in personal crime.* And further, the probability of committing a personal crime is significantly lessened in an individual who truly believes in God as compared to one who does not.

One last word about personal crime: even if personal crime never translates into other types of crimes, having a true concept of God helps to deal with it at a personal level. For example, mental health issues such as depression, anxiety, and lack of self-esteem are just a few examples of personal crimes that one commits against oneself. Having a true belief in God helps to deal with such issues because an All-Wise God discourages crimes against oneself regardless of whether they translate into crimes against others. The self has rights just like others. Everyone goes through difficult times in life. And it is an established fact that having the support of the right people (e.g. family and friends) can go a long way in helping you cope with it. Extrapolating this idea of support further, the ultimate support comes from God Who is All-Powerful. Thus, having firm belief in God can certainly help one deal with the most difficult of times at a personal level.

A fourth and final argument that we present to convince the reader that the journey towards recognizing True God and building a relationship with Him is worth taking centers on analyzing the very purpose of life. If we can show that the ultimate purpose of life centers on recognizing God and building a relationship with Him, then it stands to reason that the effort would be worth pursuing. This requires a longer and more detailed response so we will take it piecemeal.

The subject of the purpose of life has been discussed and debated by philosophers and religious thinkers for centuries. Some give lofty purposes for human life such as spreading knowledge, advancing civilization, or helping the less fortunate ones. Others have given a more basic reason such as simply living life or, taken to the extreme, living a purpose-free life altogether. We will now set out to prove that i) a basic purpose such as living a purpose-free life or living life simply for its own sake cannot be the ultimate purpose of human life and ii) that any other meaningful purpose that one can come up with is best accomplished under the shadow of the ultimate purpose of life (which we will define soon).

If we look around us at all of creation, we come to the conclusion that everything has been created with a purpose. A cow for example provides milk, a source of nutrition for human beings. A donkey serves the purpose of carrying a load from one place to another. An ox is utilized for tilling the earth for vegetation which then serves as a means of nutrition. Plants of course play an essential role in providing nutrition not just for humans but for animals as well. Even something as small as an amoeba performs the function of recycling nutrients back into the environment, playing a crucial role in the sustenance of life. This principle is not limited to life forms but also extends to non-living objects. All living things continue to benefit from the sun which day after day, without fail, serves the purpose of providing life-giving sunlight and heat for the whole planet. The stars, aside from being crucial pieces of the galactic puzzle, directly serve as guides to the night traveler. The point is that everything has purpose in the ecosystem of creation. Given this fact, how is it possible that the pinnacle of all creation, the human beings who are endowed with mind, body and soul, could have been created without purpose? This shows that just like everything else in the universe, human beings are also created with a purpose. This directly leads to the conclusion that a purpose-free life cannot be the ultimate purpose of human life.

Taking a step further and exploring the most basic purpose of life, we see that the need and desire to exist is found in all forms of life. Even animals are instinctively given to the act of survival at all cost. When hunted upon, they react with an instinctive fight or flight response. Further, they promote the continuation of life through the process of procreation. The same phenomenon is found in something as insignificant as an insect as well. It is the most basic of instincts—the preservation of life through survival and procreation.

Now it stands to reason that the purpose of something is directly proportional to the sophistication of that thing. We see this being true even in things we create ourselves (e.g. machinery or technology being good examples—the complexity of a machine or technology we create is directly proportional to the sophistication of the purpose for which it is built). And we know that human beings are far superior to animals, insects, and other known life forms, with capabilities that far exceed that of other life forms. So how is it possible that human beings, the most complex of creation, would have the most basic purpose of simply living and sustaining life? Therefore, we have to conclude that the ultimate purpose of life for human beings must be far superior to merely existing or surviving.

Some claim that the purpose of life is simply to live it. That is just another way of saying that life has no purpose other than maximizing the experience of life itself. While this is a more refined purpose than simple existence and continuation of life (because of the element of actually experiencing it), it is still far short of an ultimate purpose. The reason is that as previously discussed, the totality of human experience consists of the physical, mental and spiritual components. And the mere act of experiencing worldly life is limited to the physical because it does not do anything to address the pursuit of knowledge for example, or to cater for the needs of the soul in any way. Therefore, mere enjoyment of worldly life cannot be considered the ultimate purpose of life either.

As we continue our examination of life's ultimate purpose and make an attempt to categorize it in the broadest possible terms, we come to the realization that, at the most fundamental level, it must center on the pursuit of the infinite rather than the finite or transitory. The reason is that the ultimate purpose of life has to apply to all of life across space and time. That is, it must not just be applicable to one individual, group, or nation but rather to all of humanity. And since humanity has existed for a long period of time and may continue to exist for a long period of time in the future, the ultimate purpose of life must be equally applicable to humans of the past, present and future. And the only way to meet this criterion is for this purpose to be in pursuit of something that is infinite in nature. Otherwise, if the ultimate purpose was in pursuit of the finite, having achieved it would bring the progress of life to a halt and therefore lead to stagnation and eventual destruction. Even if one struggles to accept this premise absolutely (that the purpose of life must be in pursuit of the infinite), at a minimum, we must acknowledge that if there is an ultimate purpose that is infinite in nature, it must be preferred over an ultimate purpose that is finite. With this criterion in place, all things of this world such as money, physical power or prestige, and even the search and attainment of true love, for example, fail to meet this criterion because they are all finite pursuits. Therefore, these cannot be deemed the ultimate purpose of life.

Perhaps the one thing that seemingly comes close to meeting this criterion of pursuit of the infinite is the acquisition of knowledge. And so a case can be made that pursuit of knowledge is the ultimate goal of human life. However, a deeper analysis shows that even this purpose, as it is commonly understood, suffers from the same weakness—that it is limited to the finite. The reason is that, as it is commonly understood, the pursuit of knowledge is of this world, or some aspect of this world, which itself is finite. For example, humanity has spent generations acquiring knowledge about the human body. Great strides have been made in the field of medicine, and it has resulted in a lot of benefit to humanity no doubt. But the basic premise remains that the human body is a finite entity and therefore the knowledge of it is finite. (We as human species may never learn all that there is to know about the human body, but that would be due to our own shortcoming, and it wouldn't change the basic fact that the process is limited or finite in nature.) Same goes for the pursuit of knowledge about any aspect of this world, even the study of something as expansive as the universe, because the object being studied, i.e. the universe, is finite. In summary, the knowledge of the finite is also finite in nature, and this fails the criteria given above for the ultimate purpose of life, namely that it must be in pursuit of the infinite.

This leads us to finally answer the question: what is the ultimate purpose of life? And based on the criteria and the line of reasoning given above, we are left with no choice but to proclaim that *the ultimate purpose of life is to acquire knowledge of God and build a relationship with Him and through that knowledge and relationship, build a relationship with fellow human beings, thereby leading to a peaceful co-existence.* This ultimate purpose meets the criteria outlined above: since God is infinite, knowledge of Him is also infinite—a never-ending process that will never result in progress of life coming to a halt and leading to destruction. And once we are on the road to acquiring knowledge of the One True God, we apply that knowledge to building a relationship with our Creator. And through that relationship, we learn the optimal way to build a relationship with His creation. This last part is very important because it directly speaks to the benefit that we as human beings get from recognizing the True God and building a relationship with Him: that as a result of our attempt at understanding God and building a relationship with Him, we follow His code or set of guidelines and only through this code or set of guidelines can we truly help ourself and others and thus live in peace (thereby allowing for the continued pursuit of the ultimate purpose of life). So the pursuit of life's ultimate purpose leads to an improvement in our individual life as well as the collective life of human civilization.

It is important to note that pursuing the ultimate purpose of life does not mean that other purposes should be shunned altogether. In fact, in some cases they are necessary. For example, the goal of getting married and having kids is necessary for the continuation of life. The goal of performing work in order to provide food for yourself and your family is necessary for survival. The goal of sleeping a certain number of hours a day is necessary for the recuperation of the body. All these things must be done. The point is that one must be willing to forego the lesser goal when it stands in contradiction with the ultimate goal[4]. In fact, the beauty of the ultimate purpose of life as we have identified it here—to recognize God and build a relationship with Him and His creation—is that it actually helps in achieving the lesser but necessary goals in life. For example, when it comes to the basic goal of continuing life through procreation, God's teachings state that it be done through the institution of marriage, which comes with certain responsibilities for both parties involved, rather than do so out of wedlock which absolves one of the sanctity and responsibility that comes with the union of man and woman. When it comes to earning a living, God's teachings state that one should employ lawful means to earn a living and not usurp the rights of others. Even when it comes to something as basic as sleeping with the aim of attaining rest, God's teachings state that one should not sleep to the extent that it becomes excessive but rather spend some part of the night in remembering God. A reasonable mind should not have difficulty accepting these examples since they align with the natural principle of sacrificing lesser goals in favor of a higher purpose.

Now we will expand the argument and show that any lofty and meaningful worldly purpose of life is best accomplished within the framework of the ultimate purpose of knowing God and living a life according to His will.

When we reflect on the higher purposes of human life, we come to the conclusion that the most worthy of all purposes is to live

---

[4] The principle of sacrificing lesser goals for a higher purpose is deeply woven into the fabric of life. In nature, we see countless examples where short-term gains are surrendered for long-term survival and growth. This quiet wisdom reflects that true success often requires letting go of what is small to protect or achieve what is greater.

one's life in service of others, otherwise known as altruism[5]. Social norms serve as a testament to the truth of this statement. For example, we see that society unanimously holds acts of selfless service in the highest regard. A mother sacrificing for her child, a nurse taking care of a terminal patient, a firefighter's heroic act to save a victim of a burning building—all are viewed as the highest of noble causes. All of these acts are examples of the basic purpose of living one's life helping the less fortunate. And we as a society cannot come up with a loftier worldly purpose for living human life.

But how can this lofty goal be best achieved? The most common answer given by those who do not believe in God is that altruism should be practiced for its own sake. In other words, true and sincere implementation of altruism requires that one not be

---

[5] The human drive to help fellow human beings without seeking anything in return—otherwise known as altruism— originates from psychological roots which are rewarded through social norms. The human psyche is endowed with a need to survive—it is a basic and inherent trait of all life forms. This results in the basic need for helping oneself survive. A more advanced and refined form of this need manifests itself in the form of helping someone else survive with the goal of getting equivalent help in return. Finally, the most advanced and refined form of this need manifests itself in the form of helping others survive without seeking anything in return. All of these stages are rewarded by society as noble causes. The basic desire for one's own survival is viewed as a good thing and any action contrary to it, such as suicide etc., is viewed in a negative light. One party, be it an individual or a society, doing good and expecting an equivalent good in return—essentially a form of a broader concept known as justice—is also viewed in a positive light. And finally, doing good to someone without seeking anything in return—a form of altruism—is most certainly viewed in the highest light across all of society. This shows that altruism is the highest and most unselfish manifestation of the basic instinct of survival—a fundamental characteristic of all life forms.

motivated by any external force (such as dictates of God) in order to be considered true altruism. The problem with this argument is that it cannot stand the test of trials. For example, an individual who doesn't believe in God but has a "good heart" may help others out of the goodness of his heart but let's say he is faced with a situation where he has to decide between his own survival and that of his fellow beings. In such a situation, he will likely opt for his own survival simply because he believes this life to be the be-all and end-all of everything and if doing good for his fellow being means the cessation of this life, then choosing against this option would be the correct calculated decision. As much as we may want to, we can't label him selfish because given the circumstances, it is a perfectly logical and optimal decision. Making the opposite decision would mean giving up his own life, resulting in the person no longer being able to practice altruism at all—which was the whole point to begin with. But we all know that society would deem this person's decision as selfish no matter how logical or optimal it may be and in extreme cases, would label him as a coward. Regardless, this dichotomy results in termination of altruism, the purpose we determined to be of the highest order.

But now take the case of one who is a true believer in God (as stated above, one who strives to understand God and lives according to His will). Such a person is necessarily motivated by the teachings of God—particularly on the topic of altruism in this case—and the concept of the hereafter—a central theme within the larger concept of belief in God. Such a person, when faced with the same decision of picking between his own life and that of another human being would be much more likely to sacrifice his life for the fellow human being because he believes the next life to be of much higher value than this one. The reward he seeks lies in the next life.

Therefore, a believer necessarily fares better when it comes to practicing altruism and being able to withstand the test of trials.

Some might say that the concept of the hereafter gives an unfair advantage to the believer when discussing this argument. But as we've stated above, hereafter is a fundamental part of belief in God and thus cannot be ignored when formulating the argument from a believer's perspective. But just to keep things fair, if we strictly compare an atheist's desire for practicing altruism versus that of a believer without taking into account the latter's motivation of reward in the hereafter, we still come away on the side of the believer. The reason is that a believer's desire for altruism is driven by a belief in an All-Powerful God whereas an atheist's desire is driven by a weak and flawed self. Human beings are created imperfect while God is perfect. Therefore, an atheist's ability to do good will necessarily fail and not stand the test of trials in trying circumstances as compared to that of a believer who is motivated and supported by an All-Powerful, All-Knowing God. Coming back to our original argument about altruism being the highest of all worldly purposes, this line of reasoning proves that *all good worldly purposes of life are best practiced and reach their pinnacle when done under the shadow of the ultimate purpose of life: recognizing God and living one's life according to His will.*

The above discussion should lead a rational and unbiased mind to the conclusion that human beings are created with a purpose that transcends any worldly purpose. This purpose cannot be one that we decide to craft up for ourselves at the whim of our desires or musings because we are flawed by nature. The purpose of human life has to be the one purpose that our Creator has assigned for us: to try and understand Him and live our lives according to His will.

Finally, we will complete our line of argumentation by showing that the attainment of life's ultimate purpose, as presented above, is not merely significant, but indispensable, because both our individual and collective survival depend upon it. Recall that we previously established above that survival is the most basic instinct of all living things. So what we are saying, in essence, is that our individual survival—the preservation of our own life—and our collective survival—the preservation of our family, tribe, country, and all of civilization—are at risk if we don't embrace and live in accordance with the ultimate purpose of life as defined by our Creator.

In order to understand why this is the case, we must study the human psyche, specifically with respect to doing good and forbidding evil. In doing so, we will revisit the topic of accountability in human actions and the associated discussion around social constructs created to foster accountability but expand it further to show how flaws in these constructs necessitate the need for adhering to the ultimate purpose of life.

Without getting into the underlying neuroscience, it can be understood that our desire to do good and forbid evil is based on the experience of the self. It is in our human nature that we like being subjected to good and dislike being subjected to evil. We are also born with the ability to project this experience on other human beings, a trait otherwise known as empathy. That is, we can project our own feelings onto others and thereby conclude that if we desire good and detest evil for ourselves, then the other person would have a similar response. When we marry these two concepts together, we come to the idea of doing unto others as we would have done to us. This helps in promoting good and forbidding evil. But this is not a sufficient condition to promote goodness and forbid evil across humanity at large because it is optional (due to free will—more on this later), meaning that some people may still choose to ignore this principle and act contrary to it. Our experience supports this: we observe human beings doing bad things to others all the time. This tells us that the optional application of empathy is not sufficient in enjoining good and forbidding evil at a universal level and that some other means are required through which the desired state of doing good and avoiding evil can be implemented at a global scale. This is where we come to the concept of reward and punishment.

Even a cursory review of the social norms leads us to the conclusion that consequence—in the form of reward or punishment—is a driver for doing good and avoiding evil for human beings. If we know that our bad actions will result in punishment, we are less likely to commit an evil act. Likewise, if we know that our good actions will result in reward, we are motivated to do good. This is a universal principle that we find in play across all aspects of life all the way from childhood behavior to fully functional, mature social constructs such as judicial systems and law enforcement institutions as previously discussed. This shows that the social construct of reward and punishment is a motivator for promoting good and forbidding evil at all levels in society.

But there is a flaw with any man-made social construct built on this principle of reward and punishment: its application is limited by our ability to monitor and hold to account the activities of the subject(s) involved. We as human beings are not all-seeing and all-powerful and therefore not capable of applying this principle in its perfect form. For example, take its application towards law enforcement. If we are not able to prove that a criminal has committed a crime (the most complete form of this proof being that we have "seen" him/her do it), then we cannot punish him/her for it. Or stated another way, if a criminal knows that he can get away with a crime and not get caught, then he will commit it (as long as there is an incentive to do so). The only way to apply this principle in its perfect form is to instill a belief in the individual that an Entity exists that is All-Seeing and All-Powerful Who holds us to account for our actions. If this belief is firmly established in the heart of human beings, then they will not commit a crime. Using our example of the institution of law enforcement, we start to see that this is not just the best way, but rather the only way, to rid society of crime.

This principle is so central and so widely applicable in human affairs that it warrants a few more examples in order to bring home the point. At a personal level, take the example of sin against oneself. If an individual knows—to the level of certainty that he knows that the sun will rise tomorrow for example—that there is a God Who is watching my every move and that He wants me to be a good husband, a good father, a good human being, and further that He will reward me for being so and punish me for not being so, then that individual will necessarily be a better husband, a better father, a better human being as compared to one who doesn't believe in any form of divine accountability. Again, there will be exceptions to the rule—individuals who live a good life without having a belief system that is based on God—but when we are speaking of a system that can be used to create a "better life" and one that can be applied wide-scale across all of humanity and across all of time, we are left with no choice but to accept the fact that a system based on belief in an Omnipotent God is necessarily better than one without it.

At a social level, take society's stance on legalization of marijuana or other drugs. When society's resistance to such decisions is rooted solely in secular reasoning, e.g. health concerns, social costs etc., these positions remain vulnerable to shifting circumstances. We see this play out repeatedly: as economic interests align, as cultural attitudes evolve, or as vocal advocacy groups gain influence, the arguments against harmful behaviors gradually erode. What was once universally condemned becomes tolerated, then normalized, then celebrated. But when an individual or society roots its moral stance in the belief that God has declared certain behaviors harmful to the soul and has forbidden them, that foundation proves far more resilient. It is no longer a question of "what does current medical research suggest?" or "what do the polls indicate?" but rather, the decision is grounded in ideas and teachings that transcend the collective wisdom of humanity.

Another example, one of wider scale and impact, is that of international affairs. If the leadership of one nation determines that it can exploit the resources of another nation and not have to suffer the consequences, or that the benefits of doing so outweigh the consequences, then it will do so. We see this happening repeatedly again and in fact, is the primary reason for the wars and conflicts carried out throughout history. But if humanity in general, and the leadership of nations in particular, can be convinced that there is an All-Powerful God Who is watching us and will hold us accountable for our actions, then such exploitation will not happen, which in turn will minimize the wars and conflicts we see taking place over and over throughout history.

In essence, *every evil that we observe in the world—from a personal level to a family unit to a national and international scale—results from lack of firm belief in the True God.* Until and unless human beings develop an understanding of and belief in this True God and then live in accordance with the dictates laid out by Him, we will not attain peace and rid ourselves of evil in any meaningful way. This shows that our individual and collective survival as human species depends on having firm faith in the True God which can only result from first understanding God and then building a relationship with Him so we can live in accordance with the dictates set out by Him.

Seventeenth century French mathematician and philosopher, Blaise Pascal, argued, through what has become known as Pascal's wager, that a rational person should live their life believing that God exists because if God does not exist, then the person will have suffered finite loss—in the form of avoiding certain worldly pleasures—whereas if He does exist, then the person would gain infinite benefits—in the form of heaven (a concept intertwined with the existence of God and one that will be covered at various points throughout the book). Alas, the argument we make in this book is much stronger than the "safe bet" that Pascal puts forth. However, it does require the reader to invest some time and effort on their part. And whether you are starting this journey as a result of some event in your life or the life of a loved one, or simply out of existential search and curiosity, I hope you agree that the time and effort is worth putting in.

Preliminary Question

Before we set out to recognize True God, there is a more basic question that may be brewing in the minds of some: Does God exist? Even though this question has been asked—and answered—many times throughout history, it still remains a mystery. There are a few reasons for its elusiveness. First, by the very nature of the subject matter, there is no objective way to "prove" it one way or the other. Second, there doesn't seem to be a universally accepted definition of what or who this God is. Third, all the differing concepts of God that our society has created can result in confusion if not outright frustration even for a determined seeker. It's like having a tough problem to solve for which we can't agree on the definition, and we are all going about it in different ways.

Nevertheless, the question about the existence of God is indeed important and one can argue needs to be answered before we set out to identify True God. We can go about answering this question in one of two ways. First is what we would classify as the theoretical approach of analyzing arguments for and against it. But we as a society have plenty of experience with that approach. There have been many books written throughout history by philosophers, scientists and religionists alike attempting to answer this question and yet the issue remains one of the most polarizing of all time. A practical approach—and one that we propose to the readers of this book—is to start with a hypothesis that God exists. Then develop a criteria or framework to classify truth vs. falsehood as it relates to the true concept of this God. Using this framework, we then select different attributes that we ascribe to God and put them through this framework to prove their truth. At the end of this process, we should have a concept of God—based on the aggregation of the attributes ascribed to Him—that is based on truth. At this stage, we start the experimentation phase by guiding the reader through a series of exercises that are aimed at experiencing God. At the conclusion of this process, the reader can make their own decision on whether they would accept such a God in their lives or not. If the reader chooses to accept it, then they necessarily accept the existence of True God. If not, then their life goes on as-is.

The approach outlined above should not be objectionable to the reader. Afterall, we use it for other purposes. For example, the universally accepted scientific method that has served us for centuries and has resulted in great progress and understanding for society relies on this approach: a scientist develops a hypothesis, derives predictions from that hypothesis using an acceptable framework, and then verifies the hypothesis using experimentation.

Getting back to the main topic of the importance of identifying True God, the fact is that the biggest damage that has been done to society as a whole results from the false concepts of gods that we as a society have developed. And these false concepts have led to rejection of the idea of God altogether. The argument we are making is that if we were to conclusively develop a true and accurate understanding of God, then barring exceptional cases, the vast majority of human beings would accept it simply on the basis of its own merit (thereby rejecting the false concepts that have taken root in our society). Not only will this result in a much better society (as we will show later in the book), but it will also help in answering the foundational questions of where we came from, why we are here, and where we are going, much more intelligently.

This last statement above should be enough to convey the importance of this undertaking: that what we are proposing to do is nothing short of answering the most important question of human civilization: who is God? (And as explained above, thereby also answering does God exist?) And the answer to this question is the key to answering the three more relatable questions listed above about our past, present and future.

Definitions and Expectations

In defining the framework that we will use to identify True God, we first have to define some terms. First are the concepts of truth and falsehood. Truth and falsehood are two diametrically opposed concepts. They are universally understood and are ingrained in nature. When someone claims something to be true, we understand what that claim entails: that what they are saying is supported by laws of nature. Likewise, when something is determined to be false, we know what that means: that in its most basic form, that thing is in contradiction with nature. For example, when someone says the sky is blue, that statement is supported by nature, not in contradiction with it. Likewise, if someone says that fire is cold, we know that to be false because nature testifies against that. (Yes, this argument assumes agreement on certain definitions, but we will accept that to be already established.) Therefore, nature forms the basis of our assessment of truth vs. falsehood. To further clarify our point that nature is the best judge of establishing truth vs. falsehood, let us look at another example; one that may not be as obvious at first glance in terms of supporting our point, but a deeper look will show that it does. Say that a child claims that the dog ate his homework. While it may not be as easy to verify the truth of this statement through the observance of nature as would be the case in the claim of the sky being blue, the principle still applies. If we had unrestricted access to observability of nature, we could simply have a look into the event of the dog eating or not eating the homework, and thus we would be able to confirm or deny the truth of the statement. The point being that nature still is perfectly capable of verifying the truth or falsehood of the statement, but in this case, our ability to obtain that verification is limited. Further, human nature of the child, the inner self, also testifies to the truth or falsehood of his claim. He knows deep down inside whether his claim is true or false. And the child's human nature, in its pure and unadulterated form, would testify against the claim if indeed the dog never ate the homework. All that to say that nature still serves as the most reliable judge in establishing the truth or falsehood of a claim but limitations in observability of universal nature and the possibility of adulteration of human nature can get in the way.

After having established the role of nature in deciding if something is true or false, we should take a closer look at what exactly we mean by nature. For our purposes, we define nature as being of two types: universal nature and human nature. By universal nature we mean the physical, observable world that we typically refer to when we say something is governed by the "laws of nature". By human nature we mean the core intrinsic characteristics found in the human psyche that make us human, i.e. the ability to use reason to arrive at the conclusion whether something is "reasonable" or "unreasonable".

The third key definition we will be using in our framework is the concept of mind vs. heart and the associated concept of reason vs. belief. Reason, a product of the mind, is the innate ability in human beings to use logic to arrive at the truth. It is a common trait found in all sane human beings and can be used to gain consensus across humanity. Belief, a product of the heart, can also help in arriving at the truth but for the most part cannot be used to gain general consensus or acceptance of an idea. Instead, it can be very powerful in convincing oneself of the truth of a particular thing at an individual level, often more so than reason. To understand this further, take the example of love that a mother has for her child. It stands to reason that the mother loves her child because she gave birth to the child, nurtured and developed a relationship with the child over time, and went through pleasant experiences which strengthened her bond with the child. Based on reason alone, this love cannot exceed the love that the mother would have for herself. Self-preservation, by all rational thought, must reign supreme over preservation of another individual. However, in real life, we find evidence to the contrary. There are many cases where a mother would give up her own life to save the life of her child. And this can only be explained by the emotional bond that the mother has with her child. She believes the life of her child to be dearer than her own life. While we can use reason, to a certain extent, to explain the concept of love that a mother has for the child, it fails to fully grasp the phenomenon in totality. Belief, while unable to convince an outsider of the universality of this love, works wonders for the mother—to the point that it convinces her that even her own existence is worth sacrificing to save the child.

In summary, reason—a product of the mind—can be used to establish the truth of something across all of humanity but do so with a limited amount of certainty. Belief—a product of the heart—can only be used to establish the truth of something at an individual level but do so with virtually unlimited certainty. *So, the ideal mix for arriving at certainty of truth when it comes to things that are "spiritual", e.g.*

things that are unseen, is to have belief grounded on reason. That is, to ask the heart once the mind is agreeable, and not otherwise.

Finally, a word about expectations from the reader. It cannot be denied that human beings hold a special place in the universe. There are several reasons that can be given in support of this argument, the primary one being that human beings are unique in possessing an advanced ability to decide between right and wrong. The proper use of this ability allows human beings to reach the pinnacle of creation. On the other hand, the misuse of this ability can result in human beings sinking to the status of the worst of creation. While this ability exists in other creations as well at a basic level (for example an animal knows what to do in order to survive), the sophistication with which it is found in human beings is unique amongst all of creation. In fact, it is this ability to decide between right and wrong, which at the most fundamental level, is responsible for all human progress. The pursuit and acquisition of knowledge, for example, would not be possible without the ability to decide between the right course of action vs. the wrong one. Even intangible emotions such as love or fear depend on the ability to express oneself in the right way and avoid thoughts or actions that would result in the wrong outcome. In summary, all human progress fundamentally depends on our ability to sincerely accept what is right and reject what is wrong and do so consistently. But this requires that we rid ourselves of any ulterior motive such as ego, pre-conceived notion, or any other material gain that may cloud our judgement and prevent us from doing so.

The Framework: Part 1

After defining the necessary terms and emphasizing the importance of embracing humility and commitment in our pursuit of the truth, we now proceed to lay out the framework for identifying the true concept of God. Again, for clarity and reference purposes, we restate that the purpose of the framework is to facilitate the acceptance of truth and the rejection of falsehood as we define the true concept of God and evaluate the attributes of True God.

The framework consists of two parts. The first part focuses on identifying the faculty that must be employed in the initial stages of the journey on recognizing God while the second part focuses on the advanced stages related to building a relationship with this God.

In the initial stages of our quest to recognize True God, we must identify the God-given faculty that can help us determine what constitutes an acceptable attribute of God vs. what does not. In other words, since our goal is to identify the true concept of God, we must define some criteria for what constitutes truth vs. falsehood, fact vs. fiction, or reality vs. myth, as it relates to God so that we don't fall into the same trap that many followers of religions have, of creating a fantastical image of God that is far from reality. And the criteria we propose for doing this is use of the faculty of *reason*. That is, whatever we ascribe to God must be in line with reason. The reason (excuse the pun) that reason should serve as the measuring stick for identifying the attributes that we ascribe to God is that it is the primary tool that all human beings have that can guide us, albeit to a limited extent, towards the truth. It forms a baseline, a least common denominator, for reaching agreement across all thinking, reasoning human beings.

If we were to assume, for the sake of argument, that reason does not need to be used when trying to identify True God, then the question arises: What other trait are we to use then? Is it whatever our heart desires? Or whatever our gut feels? Or whatever our mind imagines? One quickly comes to the conclusion that using anything other than reason as the measuring stick for our initial discovery of God, leads to chaos and would never find agreement across all human beings. (Remember that our goal is to land on a concept of God that can find agreement across *all* of humanity.) And this concept of God must be in line with the one trait that all human beings have been given to judge between right and wrong. And that trait is reason.

Let us further emphasize the point through an example. Say if someone claims that a particular chair is God. Right away, any reasonable person would recognize the absurdity of this claim and reject it as false. Our ability to arrive at this conclusion results from the fact that we are reasoning human beings. Reason dictates that the concept of God, by definition, is fundamentally different from that of a chair and so there is no rhyme or reason to such a claim.

One may say that this example is so crude that it is not worth discussing. So let's take it a step further and say that the chair under discussion was used by a great saint or holy figure while conveying great words of wisdom. If we give up our ability to use reason, we can start to ascribe some divine characteristics to this chair. Some may even make a pilgrimage to go see or experience the chair and feel inspired and uplifted while sitting on it. After all, the saint did all his/her work while sitting on this chair and spoke such profound words of wisdom that it must hold divine attributes.

Some may say that the idea is still contrary to reality as reasonable, educated human beings would never ascribe divine attributes to a piece of furniture. But what if we were to replace the chair with a statue of the holy personage? Strictly speaking, the chair has more of an attachment to the holy personage than the statue since it was at least used by him/her, but there is a tendency for the human psyche to develop a special bond with the statue as it may be seen as a representation of the individual. Especially if the holy personage is no longer amongst us, the statue holds even more value since his/her spirit perhaps lives through it. As far-fetched as it may sound, what we have just arrived at is the idea of idol worship, something that is practiced even today by hundreds of millions of people around the world, many of whom are well educated.

What we have just illustrated from the above example is how, in the absence of reason, the human psyche can hatch fantastical ideas and start to accept them as true, thereby clouding our judgement. Technically speaking, we went from something that at least had some physical attachment to the saint (chair) to something that we completely made up (statue). But we concocted ways to ascribe even more value to it—to the point that we started to worship it. There is no reasonable explanation for this behavior, but the fact is that millions of people continue to do this—because they choose to ignore the God-given ability to reason.

In summary, our ability to reason must form the basis of identifying God in our (initial stages of) discovery because it provides a least common denominator for establishing truth vs.

falsehood and allows for building consensus and agreement across all human beings when it comes to recognizing True God.

After having established agreement on the use of reason to accept or reject the attributes that we ascribe to God, we can set out on identifying these attributes. The process involves proving how a particular attribute of God aligns with the faculty of reason and how deviation from it is contrary to reason. And if we carry out this process with humility and stay committed to it and not give up in our pursuit of the truth, the hope is that at the end of this process, we should—through the identification of the attributes—lead to recognizing the True God.

Attribute 1: Limitlessness

The first attribute of God that we will discuss is limitlessness. This is a foundational attribute that is part and parcel of the very idea of God. It is foundational because it serves as a classifier for the other attributes—that is, it is used to define the extent of the other attributes and thus forms the foundation for other attributes. More specifically, the attribute of limitlessness defines the idea that other attributes that we may ascribe to God are found in Him without any limits. For example, if we take the attribute of power, it means that God possesses this attribute in limitless form (e.g. to an infinite degree) such that there is nothing in the known or unknown realm more powerful than Him. (The qualification of known and unknown is important to note because even though we as human beings possess knowledge, our knowledge is limited to what we know. But God's dominion extends beyond that to the unknown as well.)

Everything that we find in the universe is subject to limits—meaning that it is finite in time and space. From objects that we create, to plants, to animals, all have a beginning and an end time and a finite space that they occupy. Even the universe, it has been established by scientists, has a timeframe and boundary of existence. Reason dictates that by definition, God has to be beyond limits because if He wasn't, then He would be just another creation and not God. (Recall that we are not directly addressing the discussion about the existence of God; rather we are taking the hypothesis that God exists and given this hypothesis, defining who He is.)

Taking the case of humans (since we are considered the most advanced known life form), we also have limits. As a result of these limits, we suffer from weaknesses. For example, we have limits in our physical and emotional strength, which can manifest itself in different ways such as fatigue or laziness. In order to overcome these weaknesses, we strive to gain support from within ourselves as well as from outside, such as friends and family or even from inanimate things such as machinery or technology. But all these things—from our own inner support system to friends and family to machinery and technology—have their own limitations and weaknesses. Our inner self experiences downturns, friends and families separate, machines and technology fall apart. In fact, a discerning study of the universe shows that *everything* has limits. This leads us to the conclusion that there must be a source that is free from such limitations and weaknesses. And this is the concept of God (in a very basic form). Unless our concept of God is completely free from limits of any kind, sooner or later we run into the problem that such a god is not above and beyond any other creation. And that is against the premise that the Creator must be above the creation and not from within it.

To further clarify the importance of limitlessness as it relates to God, we have to understand what causes something or someone to have limits. Limits come into play as soon as something is created. The reason is that upon creation, it takes on a shape or form that it didn't have prior to creation and therefore is limited in time. That is, it didn't exist prior to a certain point in time and therefore it is limited in time. (Limitations in space follow a similar argument.)

Things that are physical in nature—whether they be human bodies, statues, or other objects—are a good example because over time, humans have deified such things to the status of God, when in fact, they fail to meet even our first criteria of limitlessness. This proves that the concept of God cannot be relegated to any physical form, whether it be in the form of some human manifestation or a statue or anything else physical for that matter. Giving a physical form to God is akin to placing limits on Him, which of course would be contrary to this attribute of limitlessness. *This leads us to the following corollary: any teaching or guidance that places limits on God must be rejected.*

Attribute 2: Unity

The second foundational attribute of God is that of unity. That is, any true concept of God must have at its core the idea that God is unique, and any notion that ascribes plurality in the concept of God is false. This attribute of unity is foundational because of its direct relationship to the foundational attribute of limitlessness. That is, the existence of one necessarily results in the existence of the other. We will now see how the attribute of unity is supported by reason.

As we concluded previously, limitlessness is a foundational attribute of God. And now we will illustrate, through an example, how limitlessness and unity (or uniqueness) are essentially two representations of the same thing. If we were to say that God is the most xyz (where xyz is some attribute), then it necessarily implies not only that there is no one more xyz than Him but also that there is no one as xyz as Him either. And further, that this xyz attribute is found in Him without limits (because if it did have limits, there would be a possibility that it could be matched or exceeded). Therefore, He stands alone, without any peers, in this regard, and hence is absolutely unique, thereby establishing His unity.

To further cement this argument about the unity of God (as it is foundational to reaching the true understanding of God), it will benefit us to understand that if we were to raise the question as to why should we ascribe limitlessness—and hence unity—to the concept of God, the answer is that if we didn't do that, then God would become just like any other creation, e.g. human beings. For example, we find different attributes in varying capacities in human beings. Some are more intelligent than others, some are stronger, some better looking and so on. While we may say that Joe is the strongest person in the world, it still does not constitute unlimited strength, because there may have been a stronger person who lived in the past and it's not possible to objectively compare across time. For that matter, even if we were able to establish that Joe is the strongest person to ever have lived, there is no guarantee that there won't be someone stronger in the future. All that to say that as soon as we remove the idea of limitlessness from the concept of God (and start to put limits on Him), the whole process falls apart, and God then just becomes another creation. And limitlessness necessarily leads to uniqueness, oneness, and unity. Therefore, unity must form the fundamental attribute of God; anything else is contrary to reason.

Someone can claim that everything is unique in its own right and so God is not the sole owner of this attribute. For example, each human being is unique in that no two humans are identical. The answer to this is that such a notion is based on a lack of understanding of the attribute of limitlessness as it relates to God. It is true that each human being is unique, but the fact is that at some point in the classification chain, they lose their uniqueness. For example, all human beings are classified together as human beings. Likewise, each individual flower may be considered unique but at a certain level of classification we group all roses under the same category, or more broadly all flowers under the heading of flowers and make no distinction between one flower vs. another when speaking of the category of flowers. God's uniqueness is absolute and does not suffer from any such grouping. When we say that God is unique, we mean that there are no other gods at all. There is only one singular God, and that's it.

The direct relationship between limitlessness and unity can also be understood using a reverse engineering methodology. Taking the example of deification of a human being or an idol, we showed how such deification leads to a concept of God that is limited and hence must be rejected. So deification of a human being or idol fails the limitlessness test. We also see that this type of deification fails the uniqueness test because even if it is claimed that no two human beings are alike or no two idols are alike, at some fundamental level they are made up of the same foundational elements or component parts (e.g. two idols made out of stone, two humans containing same basic type of heart or their skin is made of the same material etc.) Therefore, they can never be unique at the fundamental level. So manifestation of God in any physical form not only fails the limitlessness test but also fails the uniqueness test.

The importance of unity in relation to the concept of God can also be understood by analyzing the hypothetical scenario of multiple gods. If we are to assume the existence of multiple gods, it quickly becomes apparent that such a scenario leads to contention. If multiple, equally powerful gods exist, then whose verdict would reign supreme in the case of conflicting viewpoints? In decisions of universal proportions, such a conflict would necessarily lead to chaos. It is obvious that a scenario such as this is against reason when it comes to establishing the true nature of God.

It is often cited by followers of polytheistic faiths that even though they ascribe to the idea of multiple gods, there is a hierarchy amongst these gods that prevents the contention and chaos from taking place. But this argument is fundamentally flawed because, by definition, the concept of God is one with limitless capabilities. A god further down in the hierarchy would certainly be limited in capabilities, and therefore not be considered God. It quickly becomes evident that the whole concept of God breaks down as soon as one starts to entertain any polytheistic ideas. *This leads us to the following corollary: any teaching or guidance that implies plurality in the concept of God must be rejected.*

Attribute 3: Creation

After having discussed the foundational attributes of limitlessness and unity, we now turn to the discussion of the fundamental attribute of creation.

We define the attribute of creation as a fundamental attribute because without it, we as human beings cannot experience any of the other attributes—it is a necessary prerequisite for human beings (and all creation for that matter) to experience the other attributes of God. In order for the creation, e.g. human beings, to experience any of the other attributes of God (which we will present later) we must exist. And for us to exist, we must first be created. Hence creation is a prerequisite for existence. (This obviously raises the question of God Himself being created but we will address that further later on.)

Now that we understand the fundamental role of the attribute of creation, let's see how this attribute exhibits itself in relation to God. The true concept of God must have at its core the idea that He is the ultimate Creator of everything. Anything or anyone else that may give the illusion of a creator is actually created itself. Take for example the act of creating a piece of machinery. That machinery consists of parts that are made of some material. That material is likely made up of one or more elements in the earth. These elements are made up of atoms which themselves are created.

All that to say that everything is created from something else. And reason dictates that this chain of creation at some point must lead to the ultimate end. This ultimate end in the process of creation from which everything is created is attributed to God.

When we look at the attribute of creation with respect to the creation of life, the role of God as the absolute Creator becomes even more pronounced. Obviously, human beings have been "creating" things since time immemorial, but when it comes to the creation of life from nothing, it is an exclusive attribute of God. Human beings have never been able to create a living being out of nothing and nor will they ever be able to. Take the example of cloning as that seems to be as close as human beings have come to "creating" life. Cloning relies on the use of elements from an existing living being in order to happen. The ability to create life out of nothing remains—and will always remain—exclusive to God.

It is worth clarifying that given our earlier argument that for something to exist it must first be created, one can make the argument that if God exists, then He necessarily had to be created as well. The answer to this cyclical question is that this definition of existence applies to things that are subject to the concept of time and God is above this concept—in fact time is itself a creation of God and everything in the universe is subject to the constraints of time. Therefore, in order for something or someone to be deemed "uncreated" and hence form the root of all creation, it must be free from the constraints of time. And that Being which is free from not just the constraints of time but from all constraints, is God.

At this stage, it is also worth clarifying that if something is uncreated, it also implies that it is everlasting because the concept of death only applies after birth (or creation). If something exists and is uncreated, it means that it always exists and therefore it cannot "not-exist". (Recall that we are not questioning if God exists or not; rather we are going by the premise that He exists and then attempting to determine His attributes.) By this logic, an implied attribute of God is that He is everlasting since He is the only thing that is uncreated. (We don't call this out as a separate attribute because it is directly implied.) *This leads us to the following corollary: any teaching or guidance that does not present God as the ultimate Creator of everything must be rejected.*

Attribute 4: Sustenance

Now we discuss the second of two fundamental attributes of God, the attribute of sustenance. The attribute of sustenance goes hand in hand with the attribute of creation. In order for something to exist, it must not only be created but also sustained for a period of time, however short or long that may be. Our existence as human beings is a result of God's attributes of creation and sustenance. As such, these two attributes allow human beings to experience the other attributes of God, hence their classification as fundamental attributes of God. (It's worth clarifying here that this in no way puts a limitation on God that for His other attributes to be manifested, the attributes of creation and sustenance must first be exhibited. Rather, what we are pointing out is a limitation on the part of creation, e.g. human beings, animals, plants etc. All the attributes of God the Creator exist regardless of the existence of any creation; but for us to experience them, we first have to exist through the fundamental process of creation and sustenance).

When we speak of the attribute of sustenance in relation to God, we mean that God not only is the Creator of everything, but He also sustains the creation. This should be clear in the case of the stars, moons, and rest of the universe—both known and unknown to us—as we don't have much, if any, control over them and yet they continue to be sustained. But even in things that we as human beings seem to have control over, a deeper look into them shows that reality to be quite different. Human beings as the prime creation may think that we have the power to sustain and provide for something but the reality states otherwise. Take the example of parents and their child. It is obvious that a newborn child is dependent on the parents to sustain and provide for him/her and cannot survive without their help. But the parents themselves are dependent on the environment and the circumstances (and many times other human beings) to do so. Even if they have the necessary provisions available to them to provide for and take good care of the child, there could be circumstances beyond their control (for example the child may suffer from a serious disease or an accident may result in the death of the child) that result in their failure to sustain the well-being of the child. This example shows that human beings, even though we are the prime creation, are limited in our abilities to sustain life. In fact, this limitation applies to everything in the universe and results from the fundamental fact that everything suffers from limitations (as explained earlier). Reason dictates that there must be a source that is not subject to limits. This limitless source is the Ultimate Sustainer of everything and is termed God. *This leads us to the following corollary: any teaching or guidance that does not present God as the Ultimate Sustainer of everything must be rejected.*

Attribute 5: Grace

Now that we have discussed both the foundational and the fundamental attributes of God, we are ready to look at the primary attributes of God. We term these attributes as primary because whereas God (due to His foundational attribute of limitlessness) has an unlimited number of attributes, many of which are likely incomprehensible to us as human beings (since we are fundamentally limited), reason dictates that there must be some attributes that are dominant over others, i.e. they are exhibited towards the creation in a more dominant way as compared to others. We submit that Graciousness is one such primary attribute.

Before presenting why graciousness should be deemed a primary attribute of God, we should define what we mean by graciousness as it relates to God. Graciousness, as it relates to God, refers to the act of bestowing bounties upon the recipients without any action on the part of the recipients to deserve them. For example, the creation and sustenance of the sun, the moon, the earth, water, land and all such things are examples of graciousness on the part of God because He created them for the benefit of human beings (and other life forms) without any effort or demand on their part. And these are just some of the things that we know of. There is a vast expanse of unknown things in the universe that humankind has no knowledge of which had to be in place for some of these visible things to come into existence. Further, it stands to reason that God created all these things and more even before the creation of any life forms so as to provide an environment for the sustenance of life. And He continues to sustain this life support system without any effort on the part of creation. In fact, it is abundantly clear that He continues to sustain this system despite excesses on the part of creation—specifically human beings—to destroy it. (Air pollution, water contamination, and climate change in general are but a few examples of excesses that human beings have taken towards the destruction of this support system.)

It should be clear from the definition of graciousness provided above why this attribute must be accepted as a primary attribute. But just to further clarify our stance, the reason that graciousness must be a primary attribute of God is that it is one of the most dominant attributes and relates to the very existence of life form as defined above. Unless and until the attribute of graciousness manifested itself, life did not exist—specifically we as human beings, the prime creation, did not exist. So our very existence depends on the attribute of graciousness of God, and this is why it is classified as a primary attribute. *This leads us to the following corollary: any teaching or guidance that does not present God as Most Gracious must be rejected.*

Attribute 6: Mercy

Similar to graciousness, mercy must also be a primary attribute of God. Mercy as used here in relation to God means rewarding the creation as a result of effort on the part of creation. Whereas graciousness (as explained earlier) refers to bounties, mercy refers to reward. Graciousness of God refers to God bestowing bounties without any effort on the part of creation while mercy refers to God rewarding the creation as a result of their efforts. Together, these two attributes provide the ecosystem necessary not just for the creation but also the sustenance and progress of life. In this way, the concept of graciousness can be likened to creation—it refers to bounties that are necessary for life to be created—and mercy can be likened to sustenance—it refers to rewards bestowed for life to be sustained. It stands to reason that both of these attributes must be present if the God we are describing is to be considered good, for goodness implies that the practice of granting bounties and the practice of rewarding effort be found in that God.

The attribute of mercy as it relates to God can also be understood in light of the concept of effort and reward as found in nature. We see that the concept of effort and reward is a fundamental law of nature that applies to all life forms. In order for life to exist, it must progress forward and not be static. And nature supports this phenomenon by rewarding effort so life can progress—effort on the part of creation is rewarded, thereby resulting in more effort. This phenomenon can be understood by something as basic as the act of pushing an object up an incline or as advanced as a farmer planting a seed, cultivating it with care and hard work, and reaping the benefits of it. It is this same phenomenon of effort and reward found in nature that translates into its acceptance by human civilization as well. For example, it is "natural" for human society to reward and recognize a brilliant scientist who may have worked all his or her life to make a significant contribution to society. If nature did not have at its core this phenomenon of rewarding effort and discouraging lack of effort, life would come to a halt, resulting in extinction. And this phenomenon found in nature actually results from the attribute of mercy of God (defined previously as rewarding the creation as a result of effort on the part of creation) because He has put this natural system in place to begin with. In other words, a true concept of God must have mercy as a primary attribute of God. *This leads us to the following corollary: any teaching or guidance that does not present God as Most Merciful must be rejected.*

Attribute 7: Mastery

The final primary attribute that we will be discussing is the attribute of mastery. Mastery as it relates to God refers to the fact that God is the ultimate Master of everything. Even though we may find many examples of masters in this world, it becomes apparent upon inspection that they are limited in their mastery. For example, a boss may be the master of a worker in that the livelihood of the worker depends on the boss keeping him employed. A judge may be the master of an accused in that the freedom of the accused is in the hands of the judge. But in all such cases, these individuals are limited in their mastery. A boss himself or herself may report to another boss or be restricted by the employment rules of the company and/or the governing regulations. A judge himself or herself would be bound by the dictates of the law when passing judgement on the accused. In short, everyone that plays the role of a master in this world does so to a limited extent. God's mastery on the other hand is ultimate and supreme and not subject to any limits.

This concept of God's unlimited mastery is particularly important in relation to His other primary attributes—specifically the attributes of mercy and graciousness. Since God is the ultimate and supreme Master and thus is not subject to any limits in the exercise of this mastery, He is free to do whatever He wishes, without being answerable to anything or anyone. Specifically, He is free to show mercy and graciousness as He wills. Taking the examples above, whereas a boss cannot give unlimited salary raises to one employee while neglecting others, God can bestow His bounties on whomever He pleases. While a judge cannot grant freedom to an accused that is found to be guilty of a crime due to constraints of the law, God is free to forgive whomever He pleases. Of course, it stands to reason that God is also just and may choose to exercise his attribute of justice in the world, but He is not bound by anything or anyone in the exercise of that justice. Instead, He is Gracious and Merciful and therefore may forgive whomever He pleases. It is His prerogative and we as His creation, dependent on His grace and mercy for our very existence, have no right to even complain much less do anything about it.

It should also be understood that this attribute of master is comprehensive in that it implies other attributes as well. And in conjunction with the foundational attribute of limitlessness, these implied attributes are found in God without limits. For example, it stands to reason that a master has power over his subjects. When taken in relation to God, it means that since God is the Master and is unlimited in this capacity, He is also All-Powerful. As another example, it stands to reason that a master knows the whereabouts of his servants. When taken in relation to God, it means that since God is the Master and is unlimited in this capacity, He is also All-Knowing. So the attribute of Master implies these other attributes as well.

Getting back to the attribute of mastery of God, we should take a moment to address a question that may arise in the mind of the reader that if indeed the mastery of God is supreme and unlimited, why do we not see the will of God being exercised in this world?

That is, why do we see and observe things taking place in the world that clearly go against what we would perceive as the will of God (e.g. presence of evil, injustices being committed etc.)? The answer to this question is that He has *chosen* to create this world with certain constraints and limits and subject to certain laws of nature. As a result of these constraints and limits, various processes such as cause and effect are in play. In some cases, this process is evident to the limited eye of the human mind. In other cases, it is beyond human understanding and comprehension. Regardless of whether we can justify the occurrences we observe in this world or not, it is nevertheless a reminder of the weaknesses and limitations of human beings. Only God is free from such limits and all creation—including humans—is subject to limits, the natural outcome of which is that we can't logically explain everything that we observe.

A follow-on question from the above argument may arise in the mind of the reader that why has God *chosen* to create this world with certain constraints and limits anyway? The answer to this question takes us into the topic of the hereafter. (More on this topic later but we will address it now briefly particularly as a response to the question just posed.)

God has created this world with certain constraints and limits as a manifestation of His perfect design. And again, this fact is supported by reason. To grasp this concept at an elementary level, take the example of a sport, say the game of basketball. The beauty of the game is dependent on the rules of the game. These rules allow the players to develop their skills and accomplish feats of athleticism, excelling one another in greatness. For example, the fact that players are limited in how they can move the ball forward—through dribbling or passing only—makes the game all the more beautiful and allows the players to enhance their skills. If they were to instead just hold the ball and run forward, it would make for more efficient and secure means of ball movement, but it would make for a horrible game of basketball and prevent the players from developing and demonstrating their dribbling skills. Through this crude example, one can see the importance of constraints and limits of any system—not only are these constraints and limits a necessary component of the system, the system loses its beauty without them. It fails to exist in its full form and glory without them. Now if these limits and constraints are necessary for something as basic as a sport, just imagine their importance in something as complex as this world. The fact is that these constraints and limits are not only a necessary part of this world but have been put into place by God so that human beings, the prime creation on this earth, may exist and progress forward. (It should be obvious to the discerning reader that abuse of these constraints and limits leads to negative consequences and we see that taking place throughout history. For example, unjust wars lead to loss of countless innocent lives, hoarding and exploitation of wealth leads to poverty, and abuse of power and authority leads to injustice, etc. But these abuses are on the part of the human beings and God cannot be held responsible for them.) Viewed in this light, this world, with all its constraints and limits, is a beautiful and awe-inspiring manifestation of the wisdom and power of its Creator. And only by honoring these constraints and limits can we partake of its intended benefit.

Now as we stated earlier, God has *chosen* to create this world with certain constraints and limits and so it stands to reason that there should be a world that is not subject to limits and constraints—wherein He chooses to manifest His Being without the limits and constraints that we find in this world. The answer is that there is. This world is known as the hereafter. In the hereafter, God will display His mastery in full glory, without such limits or constraints. Of course, one must pass through the gate of death in order to reach the hereafter and since there is no returning from death, we don't have any "eyewitness account" of it. But that is also by design and takes us into a discussion about faith.

We will be discussing the concept of faith in detail later but for now it suffices to say that the concept of belief in the unseen, e.g. hereafter, requires the element of faith. Many religionists will tell us that what is needed is blind faith but that is not correct. If we are to accept that God created us and provided us with the ability to use reason to deduce things, then it stands to reason that the same ability must be used to deduce something as important as the concept of the hereafter. It does not make sense that for things of lesser importance, human beings are meant to use reason for their discovery and understanding but for the more important issues of life, we are to throw reason out the window. No doubt that faith is required for the belief in the unseen, but that faith must not be blind; rather it must be built on the foundations of reason. Otherwise, anyone can craft anything at any time, and we wouldn't have a justifiable reason for not accepting it.

So in summary, reason dictates that the hereafter exists, it is a place where God chooses to display His Being without the limits and constraints found in this world, and it requires that we have faith—not blind faith, but faith founded on reason. God is indeed the Master of everything and not bound by any constraints or limits but we as human beings are limited in our abilities to witness His Mastery in full glory in this world. *This leads us to the following corollary: any teaching or guidance that does not present God as the Supreme Master of everything must be rejected.*

Summary of Attributes

At this point it will benefit us to take a moment and review the attributes we've ascribed to God before moving into the second half of the book. Reviewing these attributes in totality will help to get a sense of the true picture of God. We should step back and remember that the purpose of detailing these attributes is not to do some theoretical exercise. Rather, our goal is one of great importance: to attempt to identify the true God, and if we are sincere and dedicated in our pursuit, then the proposition is that this identification should result in i) rejecting all other false gods that we may have created in our lives and ii) accepting this true God into our life. Also, it is worth clarifying in case anyone may be wondering that the reason for doing this is not to do any favor to God. Rather, as we will show further later on, it is in our individual and collective interest to do so. In fact, our success depends upon it. The summary of the attributes is as follows:

God is limitless. Everything else known or unknown to human beings is subject to limits as it has a beginning and an end. God has no beginning or end. He is ever-lasting and is not subject to the constraints of time or space. His attribute of limitlessness implies that all of His other attributes are found in Him without limits. Any teaching that attempts to put any sort of limits on God, directly or indirectly, is false.

God is unique. His unity is a consequence of His limitlessness as the concept of limitlessness implies that there is no one else as limitless as Him and therefore, he is unique. His unity is absolute as there is only one, singular God. Any teaching that attributes any sort of plurality to God is false.

God is the creator and sustainer of everything. He Himself is uncreated and not in need of any sustenance as all creation and sustenance ultimately originates from Him. Any teaching that attributes the ultimate creation and/or sustenance to anything or anyone other than God is false.

God is gracious. He bestows bounties upon the creation without any effort on their part. Any teaching that does not present God as gracious and the ultimate source of all unearned bounties is false.

God is merciful. He rewards the efforts of the creation, allowing for the forward progress of the creation. Any teaching that does not present God as merciful and the ultimate source of reward for all efforts, is false.

God is the master of everything. He is not bound in any way in the exercise of His mastery. He can choose to forgive whomever He pleases or punish whomever he pleases, and His mastery encompasses this world and the next. Any teaching that does not present God as the ultimate master of everything is false.

The reader will notice that in addition to summarizing the attributes, we have also summarized the corollaries relating to teaching and guidance. The collection of these corollaries can lead one to question if any organized religion actually exists out there that passes the litmus test of all these corollaries. A satisfactory answer to this question requires a detailed study of the major world religions, which is outside the scope of this book. All we can justifiably say at this stage is that if an All-Wise God exists Who is the possessor of all these attributes, then it stands to reason that He must necessarily have conveyed the teachings to identify Him (and subsequently welcome Him into our lives). We will now show why this statement is in accordance with reason.

In order to understand why there must exist the teaching that meets all the corollaries, we must first understand the purpose behind the creation and sustenance of everything. It stands to reason that if God, Who is the Master of everything and is All-Wise, creates something, it must have a useful purpose because it would not be considered wise to create something without any purpose. Therefore, we can conclude that everything that God has created has a specific purpose. This conclusion is also supported by observation. For example, we stated earlier that inanimate objects such as the sun, moons, stars, wind, water, fire etc. have been created as a result of the graciousness of God—without any effort on the part of the living creation such as animals and human beings—for the benefit of the living creation. Likewise, lower forms of life such as plants, insects, bees etc. have been created for the benefit of animals as well as humans. And the animals in turn serve and benefit human beings, who reside at the top of this chain of creation (at least as far as the ecosystem found in this world goes). So it stands to reason that human beings, the intelligent form of life that lies at the top of this chain of creation, must have a purpose as well. And if the purpose of lower forms of creation is to serve higher forms of creation, then the purpose of the highest form of creation should be to serve the Creator Himself. *That is, the primary purpose of human beings is to serve God.* There can certainly be other purposes as well, but this has to be the primary purpose as it is supported by reason, the God-given trait bestowed upon human beings that allows us to distinguish between right and wrong, as well as by observation.

Regarding the other purposes, if we reflect on this primary purpose for human beings, it becomes readily apparent that for the fulfillment of this purpose, we must, at the most basic level, exist. That is, we as a human civilization must create an environment that supports our own peaceful existence (and thereby the existence of other life forms and inanimate objects as well since our existence depends on them). In other words, *the second purpose of human beings is to establish peace and live peacefully with each other.* Again, reason supports this view as well. Both of these reasons go hand-in-hand and picking one without the other is contrary to reason (excuse the pun). For example, if we say that our purpose is to just serve God but not establish peace and rather create disorder amongst human beings (through wars or other types of violence etc.), then we quickly come to the realization that disorder will lead to our destruction and lack of existence and therefore we will not be able to serve God anyway. On the other hand, if we say that our purpose is just to live a peaceful life, oblivious to the service of God, then it goes contrary to the law of nature where we observe the all lower forms of life serve higher forms of life (and therefore the highest form of life, i.e. human beings, must also serve someone and that someone is God.)

So given that the purpose for the creation and sustenance of human beings is to serve God and establish peace amongst ourselves, it stands to reason that since God is the Master (and therefore All-Wise), He must have also provided us with the instructions on how best to do that. Otherwise, He would not be the Master. Therefore, we conclude that there must exist a set of teachings, i.e. a religion, from God that passes the litmus test of all the corollaries listed above. Again, it is not in our focus to contrast the religions of the world and identify the one that passes our criteria as that would be a subject for a different book. All we are saying at this stage is that such a teaching or religion *must* exist.

At this stage we should also address a question that may be on the mind of some readers: if the primary purpose of human beings is to serve God, does that mean that God is in need of, or at a minimum is desirous of, being served? The answer is no, and let us explain why. First, as stated above, it is the law of nature that lower forms of life serve higher forms of life and therefore it is "natural" that human beings do their part in support of this law of nature. The rest of creation—sun, moons, plants, and even animals—are going about serving their respective higher forms of life for centuries without question so we as human beings should not have any issue doing our part. Of course, the difference is that human beings have been endowed with free will which allows us to raise this (and similar) question, but the fact is that this free will that allows us the privilege to ask such questions has been bestowed upon us from the same God whom we are questioning. As such, we don't really have a right to even ask this question in the first place. But even if we ignore this fact and claim that we do have the right to raise objections against Him Who gave us the ability to object in the first place, the argument still doesn't hold. The way we can understand this is through the second half of the purpose of human beings as identified above: to establish peace. It should be clear to the reader by now that peace is the overall desired state of existence for human beings. It is a universally accepted goal, and humanity has been pursuing it since time immemorial. (Yes, a case can be made that sometimes war is necessary, but it is justified only with the goal of eventually establishing peace.) And the single most important characteristic necessary in human beings for the establishment of peace is humility. An overwhelming majority of conflicts, whether they be at an individual level or international in scope, result from lack of humility—from a perspective that I am right and you are wrong. (The exceptions being conflicts that are accidental or result from misunderstandings. But those are minuscule as compared to intentional conflicts. Besides, even for this minuscule segment, an argument can be made that accidents or misunderstandings are not punishable anyway and therefore excluded from the argument being made here.) So if we establish that peace is the desired state of existence and humility is the necessary ingredient for the establishment of peace, it stands to reason that we as human beings must pursue the avenues for developing humility within ourselves.

Even a cursory analysis of the human psyche shows that a feeling of humility in a person is developed when that person is faced with someone or something greater than themselves, given that they are sincere and dedicated in their efforts. For example, a student who may think that they possess knowledge regarding a given subject, when faced with a teacher who far excels his/her own level of expertise—or even another student who is superior in knowledge—would be humbled by the encounter given that he or she is sincere and dedicated in pursuit of knowledge. Likewise, we see examples of great scientists who, when faced with the complexities of nature, were humbled by it, forcing them to declare their insignificance despite having made great discoveries. And since there is nothing greater than God, it stands to reason that the single-most effective way to develop humility is through the recognition and service of God. It is a constant reminder of one's own insignificance. And since we already showed that humility is the necessary ingredient in the establishment of peace, it shows that service to God is not something that is a need or desire on the part of God; rather it is a need on the part of human beings for the establishment of peace in the world and for our very own existence.

In summary, the attributes of God listed herein help to identify the true concept of God and any teaching, any religion, any creed that goes contrary to these must be rejected. It also stands to reason that since God does not do anything without purpose, He must have given human beings the teaching that is in line with these attributes, thereby allowing us to fulfill our primary purpose of serving God and establishing peace in the world. And this service to God is not something that is a need or desire of God, rather it is necessary for our very existence.

The Framework: Part 2

As stated earlier, there are two parts to the framework used to facilitate the acceptance of truth and the rejection of falsehood in our evaluation of the attributes ascribed to God. The first part focuses on the identification and use of the faculty that must be employed in the initial stages of this journey while the second part focuses on the identification and use of the faculty that must be employed in the advanced stages of the journey. In the first part of the book, we discussed how the faculty of reason is central in the initial stages of evaluating the attributes of God and presented seven key attributes that align with reason and help to identify the true concept of God. We will now switch to defining and using the faculty that plays a central role in the advanced stage of our journey towards identifying God, the stage where we attempt to establish a relationship with True God.

The use of the God-given trait of reason is essential in determining the true concept of God because it helps us differentiate between fact and fiction, reality and myth. Otherwise, anyone can make any fantastical claim about their concept of God and we would have no good justification for denouncing it. The very concept of God is based on the premise that He is beyond the basic senses granted to human beings for the recognition of things in this world. Therefore, it is tempting to exploit this fact and create some false concept of God for ulterior motives. In fact, we see examples of such exploitation throughout history. And sadly enough, followers of organized religions have sometimes been at the forefront of committing such excesses. We discussed the example of idolatry previously where the followers of some religions have, as part of their core teaching, elevated inanimate things to the status of God and such gods have been worshipped by billions of people throughout history in spite of the fact that such idols are inanimate and don't even have the power to swat away a fly that may decide to sit on them. It is indeed the greatest of tragedies that God, Who is supposed to be the most powerful of all, has been relegated to the least.

All that to say that if we don't employ some "common sense" as a litmus test for the claims made by the different concepts of God found in the world, then who is to say what is true and what is not? Anyone can make any claim about God and we would have no recourse to the contrary. Some least common denominator is necessary in the evaluation of such claims. And we determined that this least common denominator is reason: any claim made about God must be in line with the primary faculty that God has given human beings for determining truth vs. falsehood—the faculty of reason. And this is what the first part of the book focused on.

But reason is just that: a least common denominator. The case for reason is one that falls under the realm of necessary but not sufficient. While the use of reason is necessary for identifying the true concept of God, it is not sufficient for grasping His higher reality. God, by definition, is beyond the seen, beyond the heard. In fact, all of the senses given to human beings combined are not enough to understand God because these senses are meant for the recognition of worldly things. And God is not limited to this world.

To demand that our belief in God must rest on being able to see Him with our physical eyes or hear Him through our physical ears (or for that matter, taste Him with our tongue, smell Him with our nose, and touch Him with our hands) is to make a mockery of God. We don't deny the existence of knowledge simply because we can't touch it. We don't deny the concept of love simply because we can't see it. So if we acknowledge that even for the sublime things of this world, our normal senses are insufficient for their comprehension, why do we demand that belief in God must rest on the use of such worldly senses? The fact is that just as God has provided human beings with the instruments for the identification and recognition of physical things, He has also provided us with the instruments for the recognition of spiritual things, the pinnacle of which is God Himself. Just as we have been endowed with the senses of taste, smell, sight, touch and hearing for the identification of physical things, we have been endowed with the mind and heart for the identification and recognition of spiritual things.

So we must make use of both the mind and the heart to identify the true concept of God and build a relationship with Him. And both the mind and the heart must be content with this true concept of God. If either is not, then know that the given concept is flawed. While reason serves as the instrument for the satisfaction of the mind, there needs to be an instrument for the satisfaction of the heart. As much as rationalists may wish to deny it, our understanding of God is severely lacking—and in some cases can even be incorrect—if it is only based on reason.

Reason takes us to the point of convincing us that God *should* exist and what that concept of God *should* be. Our goal however is to go past that and be convinced that God *does* exist and what that concept of God *is*. And further, how to build a relationship with this God. How to feel His presence. How to experience Him in our lives. Reason is insufficient for attaining this goal. While it has been a great companion of ours during the initial stages of this journey, and used appropriately, has served us well, we need a stronger companion that can help us graduate from the state of God *should* exist to the state of God *does* exist. This companion is *faith*. And this is the focus of the second part of the book.

The Experimentation Process

While the first part of the book was focused on the theoretical, the second part focuses on the experimental. A robust theoretical understanding of God rooted in the faculty of reason is essential for understanding the true concept of God. But stopping our pursuit there would be akin to having an imaginary friend who possesses the perfect qualities but is of no practical use because such a friend is no more than a figment of our imagination. What we seek is a friend who is real and is the best friend of all. The One True God Who is unlimited in His powers, unique like no other, Who not only creates but sustains everything, is Gracious, is Merciful, and is the Master of everything. To have Him as our friend is to have it all. And if this One True God is real—as we claim that He is—then, after having identified Him using our mind through the faculty of reason, be able to feel Him in our heart through the faculty of faith. And if both our mind and our heart are convinced of His reality, then and only then can we experience Him in our life—which, as we will continue to show further, is the single most important purpose of life.

Now we will lay out the process for achieving this ultimate purpose: experiencing God in our life, to be convinced of His existence as we are convinced of the light of day, and to build a relationship with Him that brings about peace within us and amongst us.

The process for experiencing God rests on the practice of experimentation. It is an established fact, in line with human nature, that we learn by first understanding the theory and then validating it through experimentation. Unless the theory is validated by experiment, it remains just a theory. It is the validation offered by experimentation that transforms a theory into a well-established fact. And once a theoretical idea is validated by practical experiment, its truth is established and cannot be denied. We propose a similar approach to improving our understanding of God.

Before we set out to define the procedure for the experiment, it is important to lay out the prerequisites. The first and most important element in the execution of the experiment phase is *humility*. That is, the intention behind carrying out this experiment should not be to disprove the existence of God; rather, we must genuinely want to seek God. If our intentions are not sincere to begin with, the experiment will result in failure. The second element is *commitment*. That is, we must be fully committed to completing the experiment, making sure to follow the instructions completely, and not just leaving it part-way through. And finally, the third element is *open-mindedness*. That is, we must be willing to change our long-held views based on the results of the experiment. Unless we embrace the conclusions of the experiment that we arrive upon and subsequently discard our preconceived beliefs in favor of new ones, we would be betraying our initial intentions.

Anyone familiar with the well-established scientific method should be familiar with the three elements identified above for carrying out the experiment. This approach is in-line with reason, and human experience has proven this method to be sound and effective for reaching the truth. And adherence to these three elements is particularly important in the case of our experiment phase because what we are attempting to do here is bigger than any science experiment. In fact, one can argue that it is the most important endeavor of all—to experience the reality of our Creator. For many, this will require a radical change in our deeply rooted beliefs, some of which we may have held on to for decades. This is no easy task and therefore it is crucial that we undertake this journey with humility, commitment, and open-mindedness. Some of us may be motivated to experience God due to circumstances in our lives such as the loss of a loved one, financial turmoil, or other personal crises. Others may be searching for a deeper meaning of life, discontented with the vain trivialities of worldly life. Whatever the circumstances may be, in order to attain success in our endeavor, we must have a sincere desire to experience God. If, right from the start, our intent is to disprove the existence of God or reaffirm our previously-held but false concept of God, then I'm afraid this experiment will prove to be a futile exercise.

With the prerequisites for the experiment phase laid out, we can now move on to list the procedure for carrying out the experiment. The procedure for the experiment phase consists of three main elements: reading, reflecting, and reacting. These form the three Rs of the experiment. Through reading, we acquire the basic knowledge necessary to attempt to understand God and our relationship with Him as human beings. Through reflecting, we attempt to process that basic knowledge so that we can apply it in our lives[6]. And through reacting, we actually put that processed knowledge to use by applying it in our lives[7]. The expectation is that the combination of reading and reflecting should result in maturity of understanding which, combined with appropriate reaction, should result in the desired experiences. These experiences can then give way to development of new, or modification of existing, beliefs. That is, correct *understanding* should lead to meaningful *experiences* that produce true *beliefs* which form the basis of further understanding. Ultimately, we seek a change of beliefs—away from falsehood and towards truth—as it relates to the reality of God. The following sketch illustrates this process:

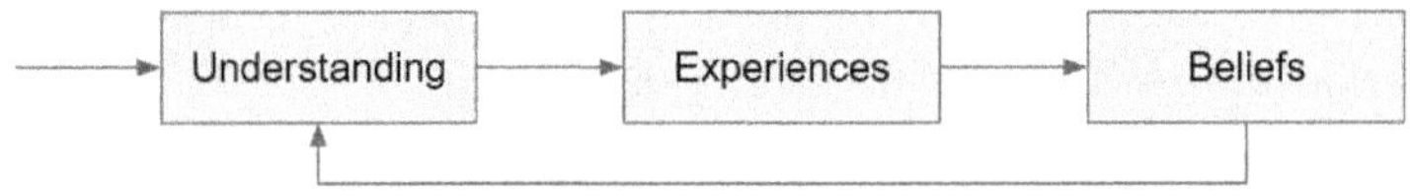

[6] Even though the reflection step puts forth various questions that the reader should reflect upon related to a given day's reading material, the overall focus of the reflection step throughout the experiment is to seek help and guidance from God while keeping in mind one's own humility. This help and guidance should be sought with the goal of asking God to put one's heart at ease and create a conviction in the heart regarding God's existence. The questions listed under the reflection step are meant to foster this exercise.

[7] Note that the recommendations for the reaction step of our experiment provide guidance around the surroundings and postures that the individual should try to conform to while reading and reflecting on the content. Research and personal experience show that our surroundings and physical expressions influence our feelings. So the aim is to gradually cultivate a feeling of humility as one progresses through the program.

The content for the experiment focuses on presenting thought-provoking facts as they relate to the human experience in relation to God and asking the reader to read, reflect, and react to them. Following are the details of the procedure for conducting the experiment:

- The experiment spans a period of forty days. It is important that the experiment be conducted with full focus and attention, without any breaks, across the time span identified.
- The experiment lists the material in a progressive order. While not absolutely required, it is highly recommended that this order be followed since it aims to follow a natural progression of understanding from the basic to the advanced.
- Do not rush through the experiment. Take the time to read thoroughly, reflect deeply, and react devoutly at each step of the experiment.
- Most importantly, always maintain the three requirements of the experiment in focus—humility, commitment, and open-mindedness.
- (As an extra, you can choose to maintain a journal, writing down your feelings and thoughts for each day of the experience. While this may not necessarily impact the goal of the experiment, it may prove helpful in sharing your experience with others or recollecting it at a later time for yourself.)

One final note to keep in mind during the experiment phase: God has bestowed the human soul with the innate ability to supplicate to the Creator. But consider the nature of this arrangement: on one end stands a human being—fraught with weaknesses, faults, and sins—and on the other, the Lord and Master—Omnipotent, Omniscient, and Omnipresent. So it is only natural that this exchange takes the form of a humble servant repeatedly pleading before a master to grant the opportunity to understand His true concept and reach a state of contentment. Without cultivating genuine humility, commitment, and open-mindedness in our mind and heart, we cannot hope to succeed in this endeavor. The purpose of this experiment phase is precisely to nurture this ability. Therefore, while the subjects explored over these forty days span a wide range of topics related to the human experience, the reader should never lose sight of the singular, overriding aim: to arrive at a deep, unshakable contentment of the mind and heart concerning the reality of True God. Every session of reading, reflecting, and reacting during this journey is ultimately directed toward this one sacred goal.

In summary, the procedure involves exercising the three elements—reading, reflecting, and reacting—keeping in focus the prerequisites—humility, commitment, and open-mindedness—over the course of a finite time frame, to attain the desired goal of experiencing God. It goes without saying that even though the experiment is timebound, its lessons are intended to be practiced for the rest of one's life—possibly starting with deliberate, repeated exercise of this formal program and gradually evolving into daily habits. With these steps outlined for our experiment, I wish you the best. May God be with you!

Day 1: Universe

Reading:

The universe and everything within it is the creation of God. All that is seen, felt, or perceived by reason is His creation. The existence and continuation of all things are deemed dispensable in themselves, pointing instead to a Bestower, Protector, and Sustainer Who combines all perfect attributes. God has created everything according to a measure and fixed its parameter limits, proving the existence of a Measurer and Limiter. The entire universe, including all its sections, is designed to carry out God's intentions, much like the limbs of a body are subject to the brain. Everything in creation, from the smallest particle to the largest body, is drawn towards God as if by a magnetic power and is naturally inclined towards Him. Heavenly bodies and earthly elements are like God's words manifested in different forms by His Power. Everything, down to every leaf and particle, recognizes God, obeys Him, and is occupied with His glorification and praise.

The universe exists and continues to exist due to God's constant support and sustenance. It is not that God created the world and then withdrew, leaving it solely to the "law of nature". Instead, the "law of nature" itself should be understood as divine action. Every particle of the universe is kept fresh and flourishing because of God.

The diversity and limitations observed in creation serve as clear proof of a Creator. The varying sizes and capacities of animals, or the fixed orbits of celestial bodies like the sun and moon, demonstrate the existence of a Limiter and Measurer. The differentiation in ranks and species among creation, from the smallest particle to the sun, also points to God's greatness, power, and wisdom

Heavenly bodies like the sun, moon, and earth were created for human benefit. God desired His powers to be exhibited through the mediation of means such as angels, the sun, moon, stars, vegetables, minerals, and elements, so that wisdom and knowledge could spread among people, giving rise to sciences like astronomy, physics, medicine, and botany. This Divine wisdom chose the mediation of means for both human beings' physical and spiritual development, establishing a balance and harmony between the external and internal systems, pointing to the One Creator.

Human knowledge regarding the universe, gained through reason and the natural sciences such as astronomy, physics, mathematics, and philosophy, though valuable, remains defective, incomplete, and subject to error.

In summary, the universe and everything within it stands as an undeniable sign and proof of the existence of God. The wonders of the universe continually testify to His power, wisdom, and providence, inviting humankind to recognize and worship the Supreme Creator.

Reflection:

How does the design and orderliness of the universe reflect the existence of a Measurer and Limiter, or a Supreme Creator?

How does understanding the "law of nature" as divine action rather than mere chance affect our perception of the universe and its sustenance?

Why might God choose to manifest His powers through means like angels, elements, and natural laws rather than acting without mediation, and what does this imply about the relationship between the physical and spiritual worlds?

Reaction:

Day 1-10: Find a quiet, secluded place during the day and sit in a chair. Read the excerpt and reflect on the questions, supplicating before God for help and guidance.

Day 2: Cause & Effect

Reading:

The universe operates as a vast and intricate system of causes and effects, a reality manifest in every aspect of creation. This principle is not accidental but divinely ordained, serving as a profound reminder that the ultimate cause behind all existence is God Himself. Every event, every action, and every consequence unfolds according to a divine law of nature, a system established by the Creator to regulate all of creation.

At a fundamental level, we observe that every cause naturally leads to an effect. This is the order that governs both the physical and spiritual realms. For example, in the physical world, if one closes all the windows of a room, the inevitable effect is darkness. This natural consequence is a manifestation of God's eternal law—our action of shutting the windows results in the room becoming dark. Similarly, in the spiritual world, if a person chooses to shun God and close the "windows" of their heart, they plunge themselves into spiritual darkness. The absence of divine light manifests as a restless life devoid of spiritual insight and inner peace.

However, the system of cause and effect also offers hope and a path to redemption. When a person decides to open the windows of their heart to God, repenting sincerely and turning away from sin, God accepts this repentance and allows His light to shine through. This divine mercy illuminates the soul, dispelling the darkness of ignorance and sin. It is through this process that God exhibits His attribute of forgiveness, demonstrating His readiness to accept those who turn to Him with sincerity. The light of spirituality entering one's life is not accidental but the necessary effect of creating the proper spiritual cause: repentance and seeking God's mercy.

This principle emphasizes personal responsibility in shaping one's spiritual destiny. Just as physical effects follow from physical causes, spiritual effects depend on spiritual causes initiated by the individual. Since human beings are inherently weak and prone to error, they are entrusted with the faculty and choice to strive towards righteousness and to seek forgiveness when they falter. A person must persistently create the conditions in their life that invite divine grace—through faith, righteous actions, prayer, and sincere repentance.

The divine system of cause and effect also clarifies that suffering or spiritual torment is not imposed arbitrarily from outside but is the natural consequence of one's own actions. Just as swallowing poison leads to death, sin leads to spiritual suffering, which God's natural law manifests as a necessary consequence of the person's choices. Yet God's mercy remains ever available; by opening the windows of the heart through repentance, one invites the light of forgiveness and spiritual renewal.

In summary, the universe's system of cause and effect is a manifestation of God's wisdom and power. It operates in harmony across both physical and spiritual dimensions, highlighting human responsibility and the ever-present possibility of divine mercy. We are called to recognize that just as we shape the physical conditions of our lives through our actions, so too must we actively cultivate the spiritual causes that lead to light, guidance, and salvation. Acknowledging our weakness and propensity to error, we must continuously seek God's forgiveness, confident that He is Most Forgiving and Merciful to those who turn to Him.

Reflection:

In what ways does the principle of cause-and-effect manifest in both the physical and spiritual realms of life?

How does personal responsibility influence the spiritual consequences one experiences according to the divine system of cause and effect?

Reaction:

Day 1-10: Find a quiet, secluded place during the day and sit in a chair. Read the excerpt and reflect on the questions, supplicating before God for help and guidance.

Day 3: Human Beings

Reading:

The concept of human existence is not random or without design but is intricately woven into the fabric of a purposeful creation orchestrated by a Divine Creator. Within this grand scheme, human beings occupy a unique and elevated position, distinct from all other created things. All other forms of creations function to serve a purpose, particularly in relation to humanity.

Humans are the highest point in a system that proceeds from the lowest to the highest, culminating in the human capacity. This elevated position is further highlighted by the concept that a human being is a microcosm of the universe. Humans possess faculties that distinguish them from other living beings, most notably the faculty of advanced thought and speech. These faculties develop in accordance with a purposeful design as a human being progresses from childhood to adulthood.

Human beings are born with innate natural states that are present from birth, before the development of reason or intelligence. These natural states are essentially involuntary impulses and responses to stimuli and help in the attainment of goals and objectives. The example of a child can be used to understand this fact. Examples observed in children include instinctively seeking nourishment, attachment towards their mother, and expression of pleasure towards good things and displeasure towards bad things. Seeking of nourishment points towards the inherent desire to survive, attachment towards the mother points towards the need to build a relationship with the Creator, and preference for good and displeasure towards evil points towards the desire to establish peace.

These natural states, while containing the roots of admirable qualities, are not considered true moral qualities in themselves. This is because genuine moral quality requires the faculty to be exercised consciously, under the guidance of reason and understanding, and appropriately for the time and occasion. A child acts based on instinct, not rational choice. The time when true morals, whether good or bad, begin is when a person's God-given reason matures, enabling them to distinguish between good and bad and the degrees thereof.

However, the presence of these positive inclinations and aversions from birth, even before reason can guide deliberate action, indicates that human beings are not born inherently sinful or inclined towards evil. A child's state, therefore, serves as an illustration of humanity's initial, untainted potential and the natural presence of the fundamental inclinations towards good and aversion to evil.

Just as all other creations have their function and purpose within the divine scheme, human beings also have a purpose. One that is grand and inherent in the very existence of human beings. Just as a human being doesn’t come into or depart out of this world on his own volition, the purpose behind his existence must also be one that is best determined by the Creator. Given that every other part of creation has a designed function and contributes to a larger purpose, it logically follows, within this perspective, that human beings, who are placed at the apex and served by other aspects of creation, must also possess a significant and inherent purpose. This purpose transcends the functions of other created entities. It is understood that the Creator, Who brought the human being into existence without any effort on the part of that human, and will orchestrate his departure without his/her will, is also best suited to assign a purpose to human life. Therefore, it is incumbent upon human beings to seek and discover this inherent purpose.

In summary, human existence is not an accident but a deliberate act of divine creation, placing human beings at the pinnacle of all created things. We are born not as blank slates, nor as inherently sinful beings, but with natural inclinations toward good embedded within our very nature—inclinations that point toward survival, relationship with the Creator, and the establishment of peace. These innate tendencies, observable even before reason develops, reveal our untainted potential and contradict any notion of inherent human corruption. Yet these natural states alone do not constitute true morality; genuine moral quality emerges only when reason matures and guides our choices consciously and appropriately. Just as every other element of creation serves a deliberate purpose within the divine scheme, human beings—positioned at the apex and served by all other creations—must also possess a profound and inherent purpose. Since we neither chose our entry into this world nor will choose our exit, logic dictates that our Creator, Who brought us into existence and sustains us, is uniquely qualified to define that purpose. It is therefore incumbent upon every human being to seek out and fulfill this divinely ordained purpose for which we are created.

Reflection:

How does recognizing the purposeful design of human existence influence my understanding of my own life and responsibilities?

In what ways do my natural instincts and innate inclinations point towards a higher moral and spiritual purpose?

What steps can I take to seek and discover the inherent purpose assigned to human life by the Divine Creator?

Reaction:

Day 1-10: Find a quiet, secluded place during the day and sit in a chair. Read the excerpt and reflect on the questions, supplicating before God for help and guidance.

Day 4: Diversity

Reading:

Diversity is a fundamental aspect of God's creation, manifesting itself throughout the universe in all forms—animate and inanimate alike. This diversity extends profoundly within the human race, encompassing differences in intelligence, moral qualities, spiritual faculties, and capacities. Such diversity is not accidental or random but a deliberate design by the Creator, intended to foster the progress of life as a whole.

God's creation is characterized by a vast range of capacities and faculties, carefully measured and apportioned among different beings. Just as the moon and sun are confined to their respective orbits and cannot interchange their courses, so too are the faculties and capacities of souls limited and defined within their species. This diversity exists to enable cooperation and shared responsibility among human beings, as no individual can fulfill all roles alone, exemplifying the concept of the whole being greater than the sum of its parts. For example, the intricate social interdependence required for something as basic as bread production exemplifies how this diversity benefits the collective well-being.

Beyond practical cooperation, the differences in capacities allow for the demonstration of various facets of excellence and power, highlighting the greatness of God's creation. These distinctions are essential for the flourishing of life on multiple fronts—physical, intellectual, moral, and spiritual.

The differences in human capacities, whether intellectual, physical, or spiritual, are part of the diversity of life and serve the overarching purpose of life's progress. This spectrum means that while all humans possess a seed of faith and innate inclination towards God, it manifests in varying degrees due to their capacities and spiritual conditions

While human beings are born with varying degrees of talent and capacity, these innate gifts alone do not determine one's success. Talent is like the seed that requires cultivation through consistent effort. A person's abilities may differ, but everyone must engage in striving to realize their potential. This diversity in talent serves a greater purpose, as it allows the collective progress of humanity by enabling various facets of life and society to flourish through the unique contributions of individuals.

God judges each person according to their individual capacities and efforts. No one is expected to surpass the limits placed upon them by divine measure. Just as a watch functions within the parameters set by its maker, humans operate within the capacities God has allotted them. The judgment will be based on how individuals utilize their faculties—whether they strive to understand God, build a relationship with Him, and live according to His guidance.

Recognizing that capacities differ does not imply that one should be complacent or laid back. On the contrary, every person is called to strive to the fullest extent of their abilities in pursuit of understanding God and fulfilling their purpose. The path to spiritual fulfillment involves humility, sincerity, prayer, self-restraint, and the abandonment of the ego, all within the scope of one's capacity.

In summary, the diversity of capacities among human beings is a deliberate and wise design by God, intended to serve the progress and harmony of life in all its dimensions. While every human is judged according to their capabilities, this judgment is not an excuse for inaction but a call to strive sincerely and diligently within one's capacity. The ultimate goal remains to understand God, cultivate a loving and obedient relationship with Him, and live a life aligned with His will.

Reflection:

In what ways can I recognize and embrace my own unique talents and limitations while striving sincerely to fulfill my spiritual and moral purpose?

How does understanding that God judges individuals according to their capacities influence my attitude toward effort, humility, and self-restraint in my personal development?

Reaction:

Day 1-10: Find a quiet, secluded place during the day and sit in a chair. Read the excerpt and reflect on the questions, supplicating before God for help and guidance.

Day 5: Faculties

Reading:

Human beings are endowed with a complex array of faculties—physical, intellectual, moral, and spiritual—that serve as the foundation for understanding our existence, recognizing the Divine, and achieving true fulfillment. These faculties, bestowed by God, are not isolated traits but interconnected dimensions that, when properly cultivated, lead humankind towards the ultimate purpose of life: the worship, love, and comprehension of the One True God.

Natural human faculties—such as tenderness, bravery, mercy, generosity etc.—become moral qualities when exercised with reason and in appropriate contexts. For example, anger is a natural faculty, but when controlled by wisdom, it serves justice; when unrestrained, it leads to chaos. Another example is envy; it is commonly viewed as a negative trait, yet when channeled constructively—as a healthy competition in striving for goodness—it transforms into a noble moral quality. Similarly, other faculties, when exercised in moderation and on appropriate occasions, become beneficial moral qualities, while their misuse renders them harmful. This understanding emphasizes that all faculties possess potential for good, and moral development lies in their proper use and regulation by wisdom and reason. True morality involves the balanced use of all faculties under the guidance of reason, where forgiveness and forbearance are exercised alongside rightful indignation and retribution. Moral reform is thus not about suppressing faculties but about their proper regulation and application.

Human moral development typically unfolds in stages. The first involves basic social manners and civilized behavior, such as etiquette in eating and social interactions, which raise individuals from a savage state. The next stage encompasses higher moral qualities, where faculties are exercised with discretion and wisdom. The highest stage is the awakening of a deep love and communion with God, where moral actions are motivated by sincere devotion rather than mere obligation or social conformity.

In summary, human faculties—natural, moral, intellectual, and spiritual—are gifts from God intended to guide humankind toward true knowledge, righteousness, and divine love. Their proper use requires reason and faith. The journey from natural impulses to morality and spiritual enlightenment is one of gradual progress, divine assistance, and personal striving. Through this journey, humans fulfill their purpose and attain eternal prosperity and nearness to God.

Reflection:

How do I currently exercise my natural faculties such as anger, envy, or generosity—are they guided by reason and wisdom, or do they sometimes lead me to harmful actions?

At which stage of moral development do I find myself—am I focused mainly on social manners, higher moral discretion, or striving for a sincere love and communion with God?

How am I actively engaging both reason and faith to transform my natural impulses into moral qualities that lead me toward the ultimate purpose of life and spiritual fulfillment?

Reaction:

Day 1-10: Find a quiet, secluded place during the day and sit in a chair. Read the excerpt and reflect on the questions, supplicating before God for help and guidance.

Day 6: Free Will

Reading:

The concept of free will is fundamental to human existence, forming the foundation of what it means to be human. Human beings are endowed with free will. People who oppose the concept of free will state that there is no such thing as free will because everything is deterministic at the quantum level. Every effect has a cause and therefore, whether we understand it or not, the cause determines the effect. This is a flawed argument because it is based on a hypothetical extrapolation, which itself is flawed. Assuming that every effect has a cause, the reality is that the understanding of this phenomenon at every level, most notably at the quantum level, is (and always will be) beyond human comprehension. It is like saying that theoretically everything in the universe is discoverable and therefore we know everything about the universe. While we continue to discover new things about the universe, scientists in the field are unanimous that we have only discovered a minute fraction of it. The reality is that the universe was created by God and only He fully comprehends it. He has chosen to expose certain secrets of the universe to human beings, but it is only through His discretion. So even if at the quantum level, every effect was to be traced to a cause and therefore deemed deterministic, the comprehension of the totality of this system of causes and effects is beyond human mind to ever grasp. So for all practical purposes, and as far as the human mind can grasp, things are not deterministic, thereby leading to the presence of free will.

The above argument in support of free will addresses things at the scientific or theoretical level which, at the end of the day, is an academic argument. There is a stronger argument to be made at the individual and social level. And that has to do with the overwhelming evidence we find in our daily life in support of free will. If we as a society reject free will altogether, then we must also forego the notion of reward and punishment—both in earthly matters as well as in the divine realm. But no one in their sane mind would be willing to do that. For example, for a killer to make the argument in court that the death of his victim was predestined and therefore he didn't act out of free will, would be considered insane. We would all unanimously come to the conclusion that the killer acted out of free will and therefore is responsible for his or her actions. Hence, for all intents and purposes—regardless of any theoretical or hypothetical argument at the quantum level—we continue to accept the fact that human beings are responsible for their actions and therefore have free will.

Finally, we must understand that free will is a blessing from God. God has demonstrated His attribute of Creator using two types of creations: one that has free will—human beings being the pinnacle of this creation—and one that doesn't—angels are a manifestation of this type of creation. Angels have been created to demonstrate complete obedience to God. On the other hand, human beings have been granted the ability to obey or disobey—a fundamental characteristic of free will. Both types of creations are a manifestation of the attribute of God related to creation.

Having said this, there are some nuances to understanding the extent to which God has granted free will to human beings. There is a balance between free will and divine decree. While humans possess the ability to make choices, these choices operate within the broader framework of God's knowledge and decree. God's knowledge encompasses all events, including human actions. However, this foreknowledge does not compel human actions, allowing for the coexistence of divine omniscience and human free will.

Humans are responsible for their actions and will be held accountable in front of God for their choices. This accountability underscores the importance of free will, as individuals must choose to follow the path of righteousness. Free will is essential for progress. By making conscious choices, individuals can progress physically, intellectually, and spiritually, striving to align their will with God's will.

So what about the line between God's will and human responsibility? It is the way of God that when an action proceeds from humans, its effect is duly manifested by God's law. For instance, if we close all the doors of a room, this action results in the room becoming dark—an effect manifested by God's law of nature that He has put in place to govern this world. This is God's eternal law. Similarly, if we were to swallow a fatal dose of poison, our action would result in our death, as per God's eternal law. In both cases, the action on our part is followed by a divine reaction that is its necessary result. This system operates both in the manifest world and in the hidden realm. Every good or bad action we perform creates an effect that is manifested afterward. Therefore, we are responsible for our actions. God is not to be blamed for our misdeeds.

In summary, human free will is a bestowed capacity within the framework of divine decree. God's determination does not negate man's choice or efforts but rather encompasses and works through them. That is not because God needs the choice or effort of human beings to carry out His divine will; rather, that is how God deemed this world to be and set the laws of nature such that the system progresses within the confines of these laws. He could have chosen to select a different system but that is His choice to make. We as human beings are simply components of that system. But it is for us to choose and put forth the effort towards progress of our ultimate goal. It is a mistake to interpret destiny as meaning that humans are compelled to ignore the faculties bestowed upon them by God.

Reflection:

How do I personally reconcile the concept of free will with the idea of divine foreknowledge and decree in my own life and decisions?

In what ways do I take responsibility for my actions, and how does understanding free will impact my accountability and moral choices?

What steps can I take to consciously align my will and actions with the understanding that free will is a blessing meant for my spiritual and intellectual progress?

Reaction:

Day 1-10: Find a quiet, secluded place during the day and sit in a chair. Read the excerpt and reflect on the questions, supplicating before God for help and guidance.

Day 7: Weakness

Reading:

Human beings are intrinsically weak. When we are born, we are completely dependent on others to survive. When we die, we are in an utter state of helplessness. In between, we progress through life and gain strength, but even at the peak of our strength, we are susceptible to accidents or can come down with an illness of some kind. The weaknesses aren't just limited to the physical realm. We struggle with emotional and spiritual ups and downs on a daily basis. Life poses challenges that can seem insurmountable at times. It can seem that we are being charged with a multitude of demands from our surroundings that are just too much to bear. Why does this happen?

It becomes evident upon observation and reflection that everything in the world is destructible. Rivers dry up, oceans recede, snow melts, and even the mighty mountains can crumble. Human beings also have a lifespan, and based on our nature and our circumstances, we are endowed with responsibilities and faced with challenges that we respond to in different ways. One primary purpose behind this cycle of life is to remind us of the limited capacities that we are born with as human beings. The unique combination of nature and nurture endows each human being with differing levels of capacities in different aspects of life. Some are better than others physically, some excel others intellectually, and others have stronger emotional foundations. Then circumstances also play a role—the environment of the household, the friends and relations one happens to be around, and the time or place one lives in all have an impact on the totality of one's existence. But in all cases, human beings have limits just like everything else in the universe. And what makes human beings different is that being the pinnacle of creation in this world, we are endowed with a unique ability to think and reflect at an advanced level. This ability is not found in the rest of creation. For example, it is not possible for a rock to think, a plant to reflect, or even an animal to ponder over the complexity and purpose of life. Only human beings have this ability and if we reflect on this fact with sincerity and commitment, the only reasonable conclusion we can come to is that there must be a Limitless Being Who has placed these limits upon us. In fact, this is the very purpose of the limits placed upon us: to remind us of the existence of a Limiter Who is without any limits—an All-Powerful, Always Present God.

More reflection on this subject leads us to further proof of the existence of God. The passage of time through history shows that there have been many instances where, in all probability, life should have been wiped out altogether from this world. It may be hard to imagine the impact and severity of various calamities faced throughout history, but the timeline is filled with circumstances that threatened the continuation of life and yet, life continued to exist. Severe famines, contagious epidemics, and damaging earthquakes, floods and hurricanes are but a few of the occurrences that threatened the very survival of life. Yet life continued to survive, whereas reason dictates that at some point in history, the sources of life or life itself should have terminated. The sun should have stopped rising, the oceans should have dried up, the rotation of the earth should have gone off track. Yet this didn't happen. It is contrary to reason that in a world where the continuation of life depends on such a delicate and fine-tuned balance of all the supporting systems, that this balance has not gone out of order. That is, unless there is a Supreme Being Who has not only created all this but also continues to sustain it. And our weak existence very much depends on the support system that this Supreme Being has put into place for us.

Our dependence on God isn't just limited to the physical realm. The weak human soul is also dependent upon God for survival. Just like in the physical realm where violating the laws of nature that are in place for our survival can lead to our physical death, there are similar laws of nature in place in the spiritual realm as well, violation of which can lead to our spiritual death. The difference of course is that in the physical world that we live in, spiritual death is not seen as impactful enough when compared to physical death. But the reality is that when we ignore the code or set of guidelines that God has given us for understanding God and building a relationship with Him, we end up gradually killing our soul by creating a void that was otherwise meant to be filled with the understanding and love of God. Make no mistake that this gradually starts to impact our physical being as well since, as we have established already, spirit makes up a key part of the totality of human existence. We can start feeling depressed, the problems of the world can become hard to face, and even if by worldly standards we may be viewed as being successful, we can feel "incomplete".

The fact is that human beings are weak in every respect and even though we may feel invincible in the prime of our life, this feeling will not persist. For example, one must think how we would handle the death of our child or the loss of a physical limb resulting from an accident or an encounter with a mob bent on genocide? In such unfortunate circumstances, whom would we turn to for help? One has to hope that they will not have to face such severe trials but there definitely will come times in our life when we are reminded of our weaknesses and in extreme cases, could feel helpless in overcoming them. In these times, a true understanding and relationship with God is necessary for effectively overcoming the challenges of life.

In summary, human existence is marked by an undeniable reality: we are intrinsically weak. Our weakness is not a flaw in our design but rather a deliberate reminder of a profound truth—that our limitations point toward a Limitless Being Who created and sustains us. Despite our weaknesses, life has persisted through countless calamities that should have, by all probability, extinguished it entirely, and this testifies to the existence of a Supreme Being Who not only created this delicate balance but continues to preserve it. It is only through cultivating a true understanding of and relationship with this All-Powerful, Ever-Present God that we can effectively navigate the challenges of life and overcome our physical, mental, and spiritual weaknesses.

Reflection:

How do I perceive my own limitations and weaknesses—physically, emotionally, and spiritually—and in what ways can recognizing these limits deepen my understanding of a Limitless Being?

When faced with life's challenges or moments of helplessness, where do I turn for support, and how might developing a sincere relationship with God provide strength and guidance in those times?

Reaction:

Day 1-10: Find a quiet, secluded place during the day and sit in a chair. Read the excerpt and reflect on the questions, supplicating before God for help and guidance.

Day 8: Humility

Reading:

The acknowledgement of our weakness is essential since it develops humility in us. And a true understanding of what it means to be human requires that we maintain a place within our human nature that is occupied by humility. The absence of this realization creates a void that then gets replaced by pride and arrogance, resulting in a sub-optimal existence (which then leads to many vices). The optimal human existence requires that we abandon pride and arrogance and embrace humility. This leads us to the realization that weakness is part and parcel of being human and a true understanding of what it means to be human requires that we acknowledge our weak nature, rid ourselves of any pride or arrogance, and embrace humility. Unless we do that, we have no hope of attaining a true understanding of God because the majesty of God requires that we humble ourselves in front of Him and embrace our humility as a seed that grows and flourishes, leading to a better understanding of our own weakness and the perfection of God.

Humility is an important characteristic, even in the worldly realm. For example, when a student sets out to learn a subject, he/she must set out on this path with a feeling of humility. If one goes in thinking that he/she already knows everything that there is to know about a subject, the effort will result in failure. The greatest scientists of the world acknowledged this fact and lived it to the core. Only then were they able to make the great discoveries that contributed to the progress of society. This concept is even more relevant in the spiritual realm because the object of our discovery and understanding is the Supreme God. To think that one can discover and understand the Perfect Being through their own abilities is, to give a crude example, akin to thinking that an ant can comprehend the complexity that is human. It must be acknowledged that God is the Infinite Being and even in the best case—taking into consideration the variation resulting from individual human capabilities, circumstances, and effort—our knowledge of Him is limited to that which He has chosen to reveal to us out of His grace. Therefore, the first characteristic that one must develop within oneself is to acknowledge one's weak being and humble oneself before the Perfect Being. This must be done with true sincerity, persistent effort, and careful reflection.

It must be understood that humility has to be practiced not just with respect to one's relationship with God, but also with one's relationship with fellow human beings. True humility requires that we reflect upon and attempt to grasp the weak nature and frailty of being human. This is necessary in order to develop care and concern for humanity, one of the primary prerequisites for progress of life in general. If we don't do that, arrogance and conceit seeps into our nature and soon we can find ourselves unable to even identify acts of hubris. Therefore, it is important to constantly and consciously involve oneself in reflection with regards to interaction with other human beings.

Some ill thoughts are so subtle and hidden that we often aren't aware of them. Even when we do recognize these subtle flaws, getting rid of them can be quite challenging. For example, anyone who looks down on a colleague because he considers himself more knowledgeable, wiser, or skilled suffers from arrogance. Anyone who considers himself to be stronger than his brother due to his superior physical capabilities, and as a result looks down upon him, exhibits hubris and conceit. All such acts can make a person unworthy in the sight of God and result in distancing oneself from the ultimate objective of winning the pleasure of God. Yes, it is important that in the heat of battle, one must exhibit bravery and courage and not be overtaken by the enemy, but even in such circumstances, one's mind must be grounded in humility. This concept may be difficult to grasp for the western mind since pride, competition, and national or self-identity is typically encouraged and rewarded, but when viewed in the larger context of humanity's progress and well-being, such things prove detrimental.

In summary, the acknowledgment of our inherent weakness is not a defeatist admission but rather the essential foundation for optimal human existence, one that cultivates humility and eradicates the pride and arrogance that lead to countless vices. Just as the greatest scientists achieved their breakthroughs by approaching their subjects with humble recognition of how much they had yet to learn, our pursuit of understanding the Supreme God demands infinitely more humility, for we are finite beings attempting to comprehend the Infinite. We must accept that our knowledge of Him is limited to what He chooses to reveal through His grace. Yet humility cannot be confined to our vertical relationship with God alone; it must extend horizontally to our fellow human beings as well. When we truly grasp the weak and frail nature common to all humanity, we develop genuine care and concern for others—a prerequisite for societal progress. Without constant, conscious reflection on our interactions, arrogance seeps in through subtle channels, distancing us from God's pleasure and causing detriment to humanity's collective progress. Even in times of battle, our courage and bravery must be grounded in humility.

Reflection:

In what ways do I practice humility in my daily interactions with others, especially when I might feel more knowledgeable, strong, or capable than them?

How can I cultivate a sincere and persistent effort to humble myself before the Perfect Being, recognizing that my understanding of God is necessarily limited by His grace and my own human limitations?

How do I balance the natural human drive for competition and achievement with the spiritual need for humility?

Reaction:

Day 1-10: Find a quiet, secluded place during the day and sit in a chair. Read the excerpt and reflect on the questions, supplicating before God for help and guidance.

Day 9: Heart

Reading:

The heart holds a profound and central place in our spiritual journey. It is described as the fountainhead of hidden knowledge, a sacred vessel that, when cleansed and purified, has the unique potential to experience the divine presence of God. This spiritual faculty surpasses the intellect and the mind, offering a direct and personal insight into the reality of God and the unseen world.

Unlike reason, which emanates from the mind and brain, the heart is the source of deeper spiritual perception. The brain acts as a machine pumping water, but the heart is the well from which that water is drawn. This analogy underscores the heart's unique role in spiritual understanding and connection with God. It is through the heart that a person can move beyond mere intellectual arguments to firm resolute faith and reach a level of certainty and love that transcends reason. The heart's conviction is much stronger, transforming belief from mere conjecture into an experiential certainty.

The maturity and strength of one's spiritual faculties depend significantly on the purity of the heart. The heart is not only a source of hidden knowledge but also the origin of emotions and thoughts that influence the entire being. Therefore, it is essential to continuously monitor the feelings arising from the heart, as these translate into thoughts in the mind and actions of the body.

The heart, if neglected, may become overwhelmed by animalistic desires, evil inclinations, or false beliefs. The heart's light can be obscured by passions and sins, leading to spiritual blindness and torment. Conversely, through sincere repentance, seeking forgiveness, and purifying the heart, a person can restore and strengthen their spiritual faculties.

The heart's central role means it can house the image of the One True God when properly cleansed and oriented towards divine love and understanding. However, if left unchecked and unpurified, the heart can become a home for false gods—idols, material attachments, or even the ego itself. This spiritual corruption can result in torment, disbelief, and ultimately spiritual ruin.

The heart's influence extends beyond the spiritual to affect physical and emotional states. When the heart is overcome with sorrow or joy, those emotions manifest in the body. For example, tears flow when the soul is sorrowful, and cheerfulness is reflected in the countenance when the soul is joyful. This intimate connection between heart and body underscores why God cares about what is within the heart, our intentions behind our actions. He knows all that is hidden, and thus it is vital for a person to keep their heart and emotions continually in check, safeguarding it against corruption and nurturing it with love for God.

In summary, the heart is the seat of faith, the wellspring of hidden knowledge, and the vessel that can either reflect the true image of God or become a refuge for falsehoods and sin. The mind alone cannot reach the depths of certainty and love that the heart can experience. Therefore, spiritual growth requires continuous vigilance over the heart's condition and a steadfast turning towards

God. Only through such purification does the heart become a radiant mirror reflecting divine light, leading the believer to salvation, spiritual maturity, and true inner peace.

Reflection:

How can I become more aware of the state of my heart—its purity, inclinations, and hidden desires—and what practical steps can I take to purify and protect it from corruption?

Am I vigilant about the influences and attachments that may be turning my heart away from divine love and towards false idols, including ego and materialism?

Reaction:

Day 1-10: Find a quiet, secluded place during the day and sit in a chair. Read the excerpt and reflect on the questions, supplicating before God for help and guidance.

Day 10: Patience & Steadfastness

Reading:

Patience and steadfastness are essential faculties bestowed upon humans by God. These qualities are not merely natural inclinations but significant gifts that enable individuals to endure trials, overcome challenges, and advance both spiritually and materially.

God has created human beings with a variety of faculties, including the capacity for patience and steadfastness. This faculty is crucial because human life is filled with hardships, trials, and temptations. Patience enables a person to withstand these difficulties without succumbing to despair or wrongdoing. It is a necessary quality for reforming the natural condition of humans, guiding them from a state of wild impulses to a higher moral and spiritual stage.

The primary purpose of patience is to facilitate human progress by allowing individuals to focus, reflect, and act with wisdom over extended periods. Just as physical patience is necessary for enduring life's hardships, spiritual patience is vital for maintaining faith and love for God. The spiritual journey requires unwavering resolve, especially when facing trials that test one's faith and commitment.

Human history is a testament to the power of patience and steadfastness. The inventions, discoveries, and advancements that have shaped civilization are the fruits of prolonged reflection, labor, and perseverance. Without patience, the sustained effort required for scientific exploration, artistic creation, and moral development would be impossible. This faculty is a divine means through which humans can transcend their immediate limitations and contribute to the collective good.

In the realm of spirituality, patience and steadfastness play a pivotal role in prayer and supplication. True prayer demands eagerness and persistence; it is not a fleeting act but a continuous engagement with God. The analogy of a beggar who persistently seeks help illustrates this well—only through unwavering supplication does one draw divine grace. Sometimes prayers and supplications are delayed, not as a sign of rejection, but as a means to strengthen the supplicant's resolve and deepen their faith. This gradualness is akin to the stages a seed passes through before becoming a tree.

Developing these faculties requires conscious effort. Patience that arises only after moaning and crying, born of exhaustion, is not true patience but a natural reaction to hardship. True patience involves a firm, unshakable resolve grounded in faith and understanding. It demands cultivating humility, abandoning vanity and pride, and nurturing a sincere relationship with God. This steadfastness must endure all trials—be it loss, separation, or pain—without wavering.

Patience is equally important in human interactions—from family dynamics to international relations. Parents often face numerous challenges while raising their children, such as dealing with their mistakes, stubbornness, or developmental delays. If parents did not exercise patience, responding instead with anger or harshness at every misstep, it would create a tumultuous and unstable home environment. Likewise, on the international stage, when nations fail to exercise due patience in conflicts, rushing to aggressive actions without dialogue or understanding, the result is often war and widespread chaos. Thus, patience is a necessary component of human life at all levels of interaction.

In summary, patience and steadfastness are divine gifts that enable humanity to navigate the difficulties of life. They are foundational for personal growth, social harmony, and spiritual fulfillment. By cultivating these qualities, individuals not only endure trials but also transform them into opportunities for progress and nearness to God. The journey to discover and build a relationship with the Divine requires patience as much as it requires faith, making these faculties indispensable for true success in this life and the hereafter.

Reflection:

In what areas of my life do I find it most challenging to practice patience and steadfastness, and how can I consciously cultivate these qualities in those situations?

How can I view the trials and difficulties I face as opportunities for spiritual growth and nearness to God, rather than mere obstacles or punishments?

How does my patience (or lack thereof) affect my relationships with family, friends, and others, and what steps can I take to ensure that I respond with wisdom and calm rather than anger or haste?

Reaction:

Day 1-10: Find a quiet, secluded place during the day and sit in a chair. Read the excerpt and reflect on the questions, supplicating before God for help and guidance.

Day 11: Courage & Bravery

Reading:

Courage and bravery are often misunderstood as mere physical fearlessness or boldness displayed in dangerous situations. However, true courage is a profound moral quality that transcends the natural fearlessness observed in wild beasts or animals. Unlike instinctive fearlessness, which is often a product of nature and survival mechanisms, real courage is exercised at its proper time and occasion, governed by reason and moral discernment. It is a virtue that requires wisdom to balance when to act boldly and when to exercise restraint.

True courage is not confined to the physical realm alone. It is deeply rooted in patience and steadfastness—the ability to remain firm and unyielding in the face of trials, temptations, or selfish motives. Courage means standing firm and not fleeing like a coward when assailed by external adversity or internal weaknesses. It is this quality of fortitude that distinguishes genuine bravery from reckless or vain displays of fearlessness.

Central to the concept of true courage is the understanding that it must be grounded not in one's own strength or faculties but in a firm belief in God. This faith is accompanied by humility—a recognition that all power and strength originates from God, and human strength is insignificant by comparison. It is this humility that forms the foundation of courage and bravery. Far from being opposites, humility and courage are intimately connected; embracing one's own limitations in relation to God's grandeur and realizing that one's own strength comes from Him empowers a person to face danger.

True courage manifests itself through steadfastness and fortitude rather than vanity or self-aggrandization. It is not about boasting or seeking glory but about quietly and resolutely upholding truth and righteousness. This strength often reveals itself in the form of forgiveness, arguably one of the highest forms of courage. To forgive one's enemies requires immense bravery, as it means overcoming natural impulses for retaliation and choosing mercy, thereby reflecting Divine attributes of compassion.

Holy personages throughout history exemplified this elevated courage and bravery by standing firm against the opposition of the time. They undertook actions beyond human capability because they were supported by God's power. Their courage was not self-derived but flowed from the certainty of divine backing. This spiritual courage enabled them to endure hardships, face death without fear, and remain steadfast in their Godly mission, even when divine support seemed hidden during trials.

In essence, courage and bravery at their highest level are not merely physical qualities but profound spiritual steadfastness born from unwavering and deep faith in God. This inner transformation equips a person to overcome worldly desires, endure severe hardships, and sacrifice life itself in the path of truth. It is a courage that manifests both actively—in resisting falsehood and injustice—

and passively—in enduring suffering for God's sake, always seeking divine pleasure rather than worldly acclaim.

In summary, courage and bravery are moral qualities exercised wisely and at appropriate times, distinct from the natural fearlessness of animals. Rooted in patience and steadfastness, true courage means standing firm against adversity without succumbing to fear or selfish motives. This courage is founded on humility—a recognition of God as the sole source of power—which empowers a person to face trials with fortitude rather than vanity. Forgiveness is a profound expression of bravery, reflecting divine mercy. Holy figures demonstrate the pinnacle of courage by relying on God's support to confront all challenges with unwavering faith. Ultimately, true courage encompasses spiritual steadfastness, deep love for God, and the readiness to endure suffering or sacrifice of life itself for divine truth, revealing itself as both active resistance and patient endurance in the pursuit of God's pleasure.

Reflection:

In what ways do I distinguish between mere physical fearlessness and true moral courage in my own life?

How can I cultivate courage that is governed by reason and moral discernment rather than impulsiveness or vanity?

How do humility and recognition of my own limitations in relation to God's power influence my ability to face challenges and adversities with steadfastness and patience?

Reaction:

Day 11-20: Find a quiet, secluded place at night and sit in a chair. Read the excerpt and reflect on the questions, supplicating before God for help and guidance. Avoid engaging in conversation afterwards.

Day 12: Striving & Effort

Reading:

Human life, by its very nature, is a journey marked by constant struggle, striving, and effort. These elements are not merely incidental but form the fundamental fabric of what it means to be human. The purpose of our existence and the progress we achieve in this life and beyond are deeply intertwined with our willingness to exert effort and overcome challenges.

Striving and effort are essential for the progress of human life, both in the physical and spiritual realms. God has invested human nature with faculties and capacities that require exercise and development. Just as physical growth demands nourishment and effort, spiritual and moral advancement requires continuous striving. Life's challenges serve as catalysts, compelling human beings to exert effort, refine their faculties, and grow in understanding and righteousness.

Human life is a battlefield of passions, desires, intellect, and spiritual aspirations. The struggle against the ego and base desires is ongoing and necessary for the purification of the soul. This struggle is not a sign of weakness but a divine test and opportunity for growth. The presence of trials and difficulties strengthens perseverance and resolve, which are indispensable qualities for attaining spiritual and moral excellence.

The divine system has not set humans on a path free from hardship; rather, it expects us to rise through these challenges. The process of striving is a form of worship and submission to God's will, where the soul is tested and refined through effort, patience, and perseverance.

Effort in spiritual matters is akin to physical exercise; just as exercise strengthens the body, striving in the path of God strengthens the soul. This spiritual striving includes worship, prayer, repentance, and righteous action, all of which require conscious exertion and sincere resolve. The act of seeking closeness to God is not passive; it demands active participation and perseverance.

Moreover, striving is not limited to personal improvement but extends to service of others, compassion, and participation in God's creation with humility and sincerity. Devoting one's life to God's cause encompasses both worship of the Creator and service to His creatures, reflecting the holistic nature of human effort.

Divine grace is ever-present, but it is activated and received through human effort. God's mercy and blessings unfold in response to sincere striving, steadfastness, and supplication. It is also important to understand that not all efforts yield immediate results. Trials and delays in our efforts serve to strengthen resolve and faith. Such experiences are part of the divine wisdom that shapes and prepares the individual for higher spiritual states.

Human beings are inherently limited in knowledge, strength, and understanding. These limitations are not obstacles to progress but invitations to humility and reliance on God. Effort is made meaningful by recognizing one's dependence on divine guidance and mercy. The balance between human striving and submission to God's will is the hallmark of true faith and spiritual maturity.

In summary, striving and effort are indispensable to human progress, both in worldly and spiritual dimensions. Life's challenges and struggles are the very means through which the soul is refined and elevated. While talents and capacities differ among individuals, everyone is called to exert effort to fulfill their potential and serve a higher purpose. Divine grace accompanies and supports human striving, turning effort into a pathway toward salvation, love of God, and eternal success. To live without striving is to deny the very essence of human nature.

Reflection:

How do I currently perceive challenges and struggles in my life—as obstacles to avoid or as opportunities for spiritual and moral growth?

How do I balance my personal effort with humility and reliance on divine guidance, recognizing my limitations while still committing sincerely to growth?

Reaction:

Day 11-20: Find a quiet, secluded place at night and sit in a chair. Read the excerpt and reflect on the questions, supplicating before God for help and guidance. Avoid engaging in conversation afterwards.

Day 13: Sin

Reading:

Sin fundamentally represents a deviation from the purpose for which human beings were created. It is not an inherent condition with which humans are born; rather, it arises from the misuse or misapplication of God-given faculties and attributes. Human beings, created by God and endowed with faculties such as reason, love, anger, forgiveness etc., have the innate capacity to distinguish between good and evil. However, when these faculties are misused or distorted, sin manifests.

For example, envy in its essence is not inherently evil; it becomes so only when misused. If envy is channeled as a healthy competition in goodness, it transforms into a commendable quality. Conversely, when it devolves into a desire to deprive others unfairly, it becomes sinful and destructive.

Sin is like a poison that undermines both the individual's spiritual well-being and the collective progress of humanity. Just as no one knowingly swallows poison, sin occurs because individuals lack full certainty about the consequences of their actions and the existence of a just and living God Who punishes wrongdoing and rewards righteousness. When a society collectively begins to engage in sinful and immoral behavior, it inevitably faces harmful consequences that affect the entire community. Such widespread indulgence in vice leads to social decay, disruption of harmony, and a breakdown of trust among people. The moral fabric that holds society together weakens, resulting in increased conflict, injustice, and suffering.

Humans are not born sinful; they possess a natural disposition towards righteousness and understanding the Divine. Reason dictates that this must certainly be true; otherwise, it would be unfair for a just God to ask human beings to avoid sin. The capacity for love, knowledge, and moral judgment is embedded within the human soul. However, sin arises when these faculties are misused or neglected. The turmoil of the ego and lower desires can overpower the light of the heart and reason, leading to wrongful actions.

The consequences of sin and vice are multifaceted. Spiritually, sin distances a person from God's grace, fostering despair and spiritual blindness. It diminishes the capacity for true love and obedience to God, which are the essence of the soul's life. Socially, sin breeds injustice and disorder. It violates the rights of others, causes harm to property, honor, and life, and sows seeds of enmity and mistrust among people. The persistence of sin in society leads to the erosion of moral values and the weakening of communal bonds. Moreover, sin and vice impede human progress by diverting individuals and communities from their higher purpose—the worship and understanding of God. This deviation results in frustration, dissatisfaction, and an unfulfilled existence, despite material successes.

In summary, sin and vice are not inherent to human nature but emerge from the misuse of God-given faculties and the dominance of the ego. They act as poisons that harm individual souls and fray the social fabric.

Reflection:

How certain am I about the existence of a just and living God Who rewards righteousness and punishes wrongdoing? How does this certainty (or lack thereof) affect my moral choices and my resolve to avoid sin?

How does the belief that human beings are not born sinful, but instead possess an innate inclination toward righteousness, inspire hope in my ability to live a righteous life?

Reaction:

Day 11-20: Find a quiet, secluded place at night and sit in a chair. Read the excerpt and reflect on the questions, supplicating before God for help and guidance. Avoid engaging in conversation afterwards.

Day 14: Arrogance

Reading:

Arrogance is a grave vice that stands prominently among human sins, second only to the associating partners with God. It is a subtle yet pervasive moral failing that deeply disrupts both spiritual and social harmony. This highlights the destructive power of arrogance in corrupting the soul and estranging it from true righteousness. Arrogance is not merely a personal failing; it has far-reaching social consequences. It breeds contempt, jealousy, and division among people. Those who look down upon others due to perceived superiority in learning, wisdom, wealth, power, or status exhibit arrogance. Such attitudes disrupt the essential bonds of brotherhood and humility that faith demands.

Arrogance can be blatant or deeply hidden within the human psyche. The obvious forms include pride in one's knowledge, status, wealth, or achievements, which leads to belittling others. Arrogance can also exhibit itself in relation to God. For instance, a person who neglects prayer, relying solely on his faculties without recognizing the source of all power and strength, displays arrogance by failing to acknowledge his/her dependence on God.

More insidious are the subtle forms of arrogance that often escape self-awareness. These include showing off, pride, self-esteem, and the desire for recognition or superiority, even in acts of worship or charity. When a person performs good deeds but expects gratitude or praise, or looks down upon those who lack certain advantages, know that arrogance has taken root in the heart.

The spiritual danger intensifies when arrogance infiltrates worship, causing a loss of sincerity. For example, a person who prays correctly but harbors pride or seeks to impress others misses the true purpose of worship, which is humility before God. Ridding oneself of arrogance is a profound spiritual challenge. It requires more than superficial repentance; it demands a deep transformation of the heart and constant vigilance.

One of the first steps in overcoming arrogance is fostering true humility. A person must recognize his own ignorance and helplessness before the Divine. Humbleness is described as a seed for faith, and faith itself is essential for liberation from sin, including arrogance.

Self-awareness is crucial—acknowledging subtle arrogant tendencies allows one to combat them effectively. Since arrogance often disguises itself as confidence or rightful pride, continuous self-examination and sincerity in repentance are necessary.

Moreover, arrogance can only be truly overcome by cultivating love and devotion to God. The true lover of God loses himself in the Beloved, reflecting divine qualities rather than seeking self-exaltation. This love softens the heart, replacing arrogance with humility and sincere service to others. This love and devotion to God must be accompanied with righteous conduct in order to fight against arrogance. This includes abandoning major sins like adultery and theft, as well as the more subtle vices of scorn, jealousy, and impatience. True righteousness involves being mindful of all trusts and covenants, both with God and fellow human beings.

In summary, arrogance is a formidable barrier on the spiritual path, second only to idolatry or association with God in its gravity. It manifests in both overt and covert ways, corrupting the heart and disrupting relationships. Overcoming arrogance demands humility, sincere repentance, love for God, and a commitment to righteousness. It is a continuous struggle to subdue the ego and cultivate a heart that is wholly devoted to God alone.

Reflection:

In what ways might I be unknowingly harboring subtle forms of arrogance, such as pride in my actions or the desire for recognition, even in my worship or charity?

Do my actions and attitudes reflect love and devotion to God that soften my heart and replace arrogance with sincere service to others?

Reaction:

Day 11-20: Find a quiet, secluded place at night and sit in a chair. Read the excerpt and reflect on the questions, supplicating before God for help and guidance. Avoid engaging in conversation afterwards.

Day 15: Greed

Reading:

Greed, fundamentally, arises from an unquenchable desire to hoard wealth. It is not merely the pursuit of financial stability or comfort but an insatiable craving for more, beyond what is necessary for a comfortable lifestyle. We witness this vividly in the modern world, where the richest people possess wealth that far exceeds their needs, yet their desire for accumulation continues unabated. This phenomenon is not accidental but deeply rooted in society's collective mindset that equates greater wealth with greater deservingness.

Society often views the accumulation of wealth as a mark of success and virtue, fostering a culture where the goal becomes amassing more, irrespective of the means. The concept of working hard to make money is frequently considered in a vacuum, emphasizing only the positive aspects of industriousness and ignoring the potential harm caused by such pursuits. This selective focus results in an implicit acceptance—or at least a lack of scrutiny—of making money at the expense of others. The negative consequences, such as exploitation or social inequality, are often overlooked or minimized because they are perceived as incidental to the positive goal of economic progress.

Indeed, greed is one of the root causes of the vast inequality seen in the world today. The disproportionate concentration of wealth in the hands of a few not only widens the economic gap but also erodes the moral fabric of society. However, from a spiritual perspective, God does not regard the riches of this world as holding any value. What holds significance is what resides in one's heart—humility, sincerity, and kindness. Prosperity and wealth are not ultimate ends but means, and their spiritual worth depends on the attitude and intentions with which they are acquired and used.

This is not to suggest that God opposes human striving or ambition. On the contrary, the progress of humanity is fundamentally based on striving. The difference, however, lies in the purpose and balance of this striving. It should be directed towards good, maintaining equilibrium between one's rights and the rights of others, and not towards accumulating wealth and riches solely for the sake of oneself, blinded by greed and unconcerned with basic human values. True striving recognizes that all physical, mental, and spiritual capabilities, including wealth and other worldly possessions, are ultimately bestowed by God. He is the Source and Bestower of all bounties, and acknowledging this underpins a healthy relationship with material wealth.

Greed and miserliness represent significant spiritual impediments. They emerge from an excessive attachment to worldly possessions and self-centered desires. Such attachments hinder a person's connection with God and obstruct the attainment of higher moral and spiritual states. The misuse of human faculties corrupts natural qualities, turning what could be beneficial into harmful traits. For instance, while envy can be a competitive drive towards goodness, its misuse renders it destructive.

In contrast, righteousness and spiritual progress involve honesty, generosity, and balance—recognizing wealth as a trust from God. The spiritual path requires one to overcome the poison of greed through humility, repentance, and sincere striving towards goodness. Only then can a person achieve the true prosperity that begins in this life and culminates in the hereafter.

In summary, greed fundamentally stems from an insatiable desire to accumulate wealth beyond what is necessary, reflecting a societal mindset that equates wealth with worthiness and success. This cultural attitude fosters a relentless pursuit of money often without regard for the means employed, leading to exploitation and widening social inequalities. Human striving is essential but must be balanced and directed toward good, acknowledging God as the ultimate source of all blessings. Greed blinds the individual to the true purpose of life, which is the worship, understanding, and love of God and love for His creation. The remedy lies in recognizing that all wealth is transient and that the real treasure is a heart aligned with divine will—driven towards progress but humble and generous in its pursuit.

Reflection:

How do my attitudes toward wealth and material possessions reflect my understanding of their true purpose and origin?

Do I recognize God as the ultimate Source and Bestower of all bounties in my life?

How do I guard against the spiritual impediments of greed and miserliness in my daily life?

Reaction:

Day 11-20: Find a quiet, secluded place at night and sit in a chair. Read the excerpt and reflect on the questions, supplicating before God for help and guidance. Avoid engaging in conversation afterwards.

Day 16: Truthfulness

Reading:

Truthfulness is a fundamental moral quality intimately connected with human nature. At its core, truthfulness is the sincere declaration and acceptance of reality as it is, free from deceit or falsehood. It is not merely the absence of lying but encompasses a deep alignment of one's words and actions with reality and conscience. In human nature, truthfulness is evident in an innate aversion to falsehood. Even infants, in their simplicity and naivety, instinctively reject what belongs to others, mirroring the root cause of honesty and integrity. However, this natural aversion alone does not constitute full-fledged morality; full truthfulness requires the conscious and reasoned exercise of this inclination, especially under challenging circumstances where telling the truth may involve risk or sacrifice.

Truth manifests itself abundantly and self-evidently in nature. The universe operates according to precise laws and orders that are consistent and reliable, revealing an underlying reality that is clear and unmistakable to reason. For example, natural faculties such as sight and hearing depend on physical realities like light and sound, which exist independently and objectively. Similarly, human faculties and natural laws operate in harmony with truth, reflecting a universal order established by God. This orderliness and the consistent functioning of natural laws serve as a testament to the reality and primacy of truth in the universe.

Developing the habit of telling the truth involves more than mere adherence to external rules; it requires cultivating an inner disposition grounded in sincerity and conscience. One must nurture a deep dislike and abhorrence for falsehood akin to the infant's aversion to what belongs to others. This moral quality emerges fully when reason and reflection guide a person to value truth not only when it is easy but also when it is costly or difficult to uphold. Repentance and sincere resolve to abandon falsehood are vital elements in this moral reform, enabling individuals to progress from natural inclination to conscious moral commitment.

Telling the truth aligns harmoniously with human nature and the universal nature of things. Just as natural faculties and actions have inherent purposes—eyes for seeing, ears for hearing—truthfulness serves as a natural moral faculty that brings harmony to human interactions and society. Acting truthfully is consistent with the innate human tendency towards sincerity and integrity, and it supports the social fabric by fostering trust and cooperation. Hence, truthfulness is not only a personal virtue but an essential element of universal natural law. Human nature and universal nature both support truth and repel falsehood.

God, the Creator of all, profoundly values truth and detests falsehood. Divine attributes are perfect and free from defect, and God's knowledge is complete and absolute, encompassing all realities without distance or barrier. In accordance with His nature, God's law and justice favor truthfulness, rewarding those who uphold it and warning against deceit. The acceptance of truth is also a gateway to divine knowledge and grace, as faith—rooted in truthful acceptance of the known and the unknown—opens the heart to higher understanding and spiritual illumination. Thus, truthfulness is not only favored but is a means through which humans draw nearer to God.

In summary, truthfulness is a natural and moral quality deeply embedded in human nature and reflected universally in the natural order that we find in the universe. It is a habit to be cultivated through conscious effort and sincerity, aligning human conduct with divine will. Upholding truth is essential for individual moral growth, social harmony, and spiritual proximity to God.

Reflection:

In what ways do I naturally demonstrate truthfulness in my daily life, and where might I be falling short, especially when honesty is difficult or costly?

In what ways does my relationship with truthfulness affect my spiritual growth and closeness to God, considering that truth is a gateway to divine knowledge and grace?

Reaction:

Day 11-20: Find a quiet, secluded place at night and sit in a chair. Read the excerpt and reflect on the questions, supplicating before God for help and guidance. Avoid engaging in conversation afterwards.

Day 17: Falsehood

Reading:

Falsehood, in its essence, is the deliberate deviation from truth, a misrepresentation that obscures reality and sows discord in human relations and spiritual life. It is not merely the utterance of untruths but encompasses any act or state that distances a person from sincerity, integrity, and moral rectitude.

Falsehood may be understood as the absence or negation of truthfulness, characterized by dishonesty, deceit, and insincerity. It is a moral failing where an individual deliberately misleads others or himself, departing from the natural state of honesty that is innate in human beings.

Falsehood arises from the misuse of human faculties and natural qualities. While honesty and truthfulness are natural states embedded in the human soul, the presence of selfish motives and the overpowering of reason by lower impulses lead to falsehood. It is not an inherent trait but a deviation stemming from human weakness and the dominance of egoistic desires. The soul, created by God and invested with faculties of comprehension and moral discrimination, can be veiled by passions and animalistic tendencies, which lead to dishonesty and falsehood.

Several causes compel human beings to resort to falsehood. Chief among these is the weakness of human nature and the influence of the ego that incites evil. When a person is threatened in life, property, or honor, or driven by selfish interests, the natural inclination to truthfulness may be abandoned. The lack of perfect understanding of God and the absence of certainty in divine accountability further embolden individuals to lie and deceive, as they do not fear any ultimate consequence. Moreover, vices like arrogance, pride, and self-esteem can blind a person to the harm of falsehood, leading to its proliferation in social conduct.

To avoid falsehood, one must nurture and strengthen the natural inclination towards honesty through the guidance of reason and spiritual understanding. Moral qualities emerge fully when exercised with prudence, at the right time and place, and under the control of divine wisdom. This requires the cultivation of sincerity, humility, repentance, and steadfastness in righteousness. The recognition of God, faith in His existence and attributes, and the fear of divine punishment serve as strong deterrents against falsehood. Repentance and seeking forgiveness are vital instruments for moral reform and cleansing from the stain of falsehood.

God, the fountainhead of all perfection and truth, inherently dislikes falsehood. Falsehood is a deviation from the divine attributes of mercy, justice, and truth. God is Most Forgiving and Merciful but also demands sincerity and truthfulness from His servants. To please God and attain nearness to Him, a person must develop perfect faith, humility, and love for God, which naturally manifest in truthfulness and avoidance of falsehood.

In summary, falsehood is a moral disease that originates from the misuse of human faculties and the dominance of selfish desires.

It contrasts sharply with the innate human disposition towards honesty and integrity, which must be nurtured through reason, faith, and spiritual discipline. Avoiding falsehood requires a deep recognition of God's attributes, sincere repentance, and steadfastness in righteousness. Pleasing God and drawing near to Him is inseparable from truthfulness, humility, and sincere worship. Thus, the journey towards God is a journey away from falsehood and towards the light of truth and divine love.

Reflection:

How can I cultivate a deeper inner aversion to falsehood, similar to the innate instinct seen even in infants, and transform this into a conscious moral commitment?

How can I convince myself that falsehood is a moral disease and not a natural faculty?

Reaction:

Day 11-20: Find a quiet, secluded place at night and sit in a chair. Read the excerpt and reflect on the questions, supplicating before God for help and guidance. Avoid engaging in conversation afterwards.

Day 18: Knowledge

Reading:

Human knowledge and the pursuit of learning have always been central to our progress and development. From the earliest discoveries to modern technological marvels, the journey of human intellect is deeply intertwined with divine wisdom and the limitations inherent in our nature. An exploration of this journey reveals profound insights about the source of true knowledge, the role of human endeavors, and the divine providence that guides spiritual and intellectual growth.

Human knowledge is inherently limited and often incomplete. Without divine guidance, reason alone can mislead, leading some to atheism or error in understanding the unseen realities of existence. Knowledge acquired purely through human faculties, devoid of divine revelation, remains speculative and can result in misguided beliefs and practices. This underscores the necessity of humility, supplication, and divine assistance in the pursuit of knowledge.

The knowledge possessed by God is perfect, absolute, and infinite, surpassing all human understanding. Unlike human knowledge, which is partial, limited, and prone to error, God's knowledge is perfect, the totality of which is beyond human comprehension. It is the highest and most certain knowledge, encompassing every particle and event in the universe without deficiency or compulsion. In contrast, human intellect can only grasp a fraction of reality and is incapable of fully comprehending divine activities or the entirety of creation.

True knowledge originates solely from God, Who chooses to bestow it upon humans according to His wishes. While humans possess faculties for learning and reflection, the ultimate illumination comes from divine revelation and inspiration. God has endowed humans with intellectual faculties of the brain as well as spiritual faculties of the heart, the latter being the source of hidden knowledge and understanding beyond mere reason. This divine bestowal is not uniform; it varies according to the capacity, sincerity, and spiritual rank of the individual, highlighting the diversity of human intellectual and spiritual potential.

Inventions and technological advancements are manifestations of human capacity to reflect, reason, and make use of God-given faculties. Just as inventors harness natural forces—like steam to power locomotives—they operate within the limits set by God, Who has created capacities and imposed boundaries on all created beings. For example, the moon and the sun follow fixed orbits determined by divine ordinance, and human physicians cannot alter the inherent capacities of bodies beyond their natural limits. Thus, inventions arise when humans employ their faculties within the framework of divine law and natural order.

The pursuit of knowledge enlightens the human mind and elevates the soul. Rational reflection, combined with revelation, leads to certainty and spiritual insight. Knowledge nurtures understanding, which is essential for moral development and the recognition of God. The process of acquiring knowledge from childhood through adulthood mirrors the spiritual journey from rudimentary moral awareness to higher stages of moral and spiritual maturity. As individuals progress intellectually and spiritually, they become capable of deeper comprehension, righteous conduct, and love for the Divine.

Human development—physical, intellectual, and spiritual—occurs in stages. Initially, humans acquire basic cultural and moral behaviors that differentiate them from animals. Subsequently, they ascend to higher moral stages marked by self-reproach, understanding, and devotion to God. This progression reflects the divine design where natural faculties and moral consciousness mature gradually, culminating in spiritual enlightenment and nearness to God.

Reflection plays a crucial role in enabling and nurturing the human mind. God has endowed human reason with the ability to think, plan, and devise means for success in both good and bad designs. Intellectual faculties, when combined with divine inspiration, empower humans to uncover hidden truths and create solutions that advance civilization. However, such intellectual activity must be guided by righteousness and humility to avoid misguidance.

God reveals hidden knowledge about the universe progressively, according to the time, need, and capacity of humanity. This revelation sustains human progress and spiritual evolution. The divine law ensures that spiritual insights and scientific knowledge are not static but unfold gradually, allowing humankind to adapt and grow. Such unfolding of knowledge confirms the continuous mercy and grace of God, Who desires human beings to attain understanding and salvation through both natural faculties and supernatural guidance.

In summary, human knowledge, inventions, and progress are deeply connected to the divine wisdom and the faculties bestowed by God. Our limited intellect and capacities are complemented by revelation and spiritual insight, guiding us towards moral maturity and true understanding. While inventions spring from the use of God-given faculties within natural limits, the ultimate source of knowledge remains God, Who reveals His secrets progressively to humanity for its benefit and salvation.

Reflection:

In what ways do I cultivate humility and sincerity in my quest for knowledge, acknowledging that true understanding is ultimately a gift from God?

Reflecting on the stages of development of collective human knowledge, do I understand the wisdom behind application of this knowledge for the propagation of God's message?

Reaction:

Day 11-20: Find a quiet, secluded place at night and sit in a chair. Read the excerpt and reflect on the questions, supplicating before God for help and guidance. Avoid engaging in conversation afterwards.

Day 19: Reason

Reading:

Human reason is a profound gift bestowed upon humankind by God. It serves as the cornerstone of human comprehension, enabling individuals to reflect, deliberate, and seek understanding about the world and beyond. However, the ability to reason, while vital, has its bounds, especially when it comes to the knowledge of the Divine.

Reason is an inherent faculty given by God to humans. It is not a mere accidental attribute, but a deliberate endowment designed to allow humans to discern truth and distinguish right from wrong. God invested human beings with an advanced faculty of comprehension so that humans could understand and worship Him and learn to live in peace with each other. This endowment is part of the very nature of human beings, enabling them to seek knowledge and to progress forward.

The benefits of reason are numerous and foundational to human advancement. Amongst other things, reason allows us to recognize the existence of the Creator by contemplating His perfect and orderly creation, distinguish between good and evil thus laying the groundwork for moral development, acquire knowledge through observation, experience, and history, and guide human behavior and social interaction toward civilization and culture.

Despite its importance, reason has intrinsic limitations, especially in matters beyond the physical and observable world. Reason alone can only establish the necessity or possibility of the existence of God but cannot achieve the certainty of His existence. Human reason is incapable of perceiving the unseen and metaphysical realities, such as the soul's journey after death or the full attributes of God.

Philosophers and scientists who relied solely on reason often ended up in atheism or skepticism because reason could not conclusively prove spiritual truths. Despite their deep engagement with astronomy, physics, and philosophy, they failed to attain certainty about God and the soul. Their reliance on reason alone led them to doubts, errors, and ultimately atheism. They rejected spiritual realities such as angels, revelation, and the afterlife because these do not fall within the realm of empirical verification

Not every human being is endowed with reason in the same measure. There is a broad spectrum of intellectual and spiritual faculties among people. Some possess highly developed faculties, allowing them to comprehend and reflect deeply, while others have more limited capacities. Human beings vary greatly in their stages of understanding, righteousness, fear of God, and divine love, confirming that reason is not uniformly distributed. This diversity implies that guidance is tailored to the capacities of individuals. And God will judge individuals based on their effort keeping in mind the capacities bestowed upon them.

In summary, reason is a divinely granted faculty that enables humans to recognize God's existence, develop morality, and pursue knowledge. It is indispensable for intellectual and spiritual progress.

However, reason alone is insufficient for attaining full certainty about the divine and metaphysical realities. It varies in quality and quantity among individuals, reflecting the diversity of human capacities. Ultimately, reason must be complemented by faith, which confirms and fulfills the aspirations of the intellect and heart in the journey toward understanding God and achieving salvation.

Reflection:

How do I currently use reason to contemplate the existence and attributes of God, and where do I find its limitations in reaching certainty about spiritual truths?

How can I balance the use of reason with faith in my personal journey toward understanding God and moral development?

Reflecting on the fact that reason alone cannot perceive the unseen, how open am I to complementary sources of knowledge like revelation and spiritual insight in my quest for truth?

Reaction:

Day 11-20: Find a quiet, secluded place at night and sit in a chair. Read the excerpt and reflect on the questions, supplicating before God for help and guidance. Avoid engaging in conversation afterwards.

Day 20: Faith

Reading:

Faith can be defined as a profound and sincere acceptance of realities that transcend immediate human perception—belief in the unseen and the unknown. It is not acceptance of tales or unproven stories, but a reasoned conviction grounded in evidence, experience, and divine inspiration. True faith is essential for human beings to achieve spiritual certainty and salvation, forming the foundation of a meaningful, purposeful life.

Faith involves accepting truths that are not directly observable or fully comprehensible through human senses or reason alone. It demands belief in the unseen—God's existence, His perfect attributes, the afterlife, angels, and other metaphysical realities. These truths may initially be accepted on the basis of reason but should ultimately lead to certainty through spiritual insight and divine guidance. Reason without faith can lead one to atheism, while faith that is not based on sound reason can lead to fanaticism. It is only faith grounded in reason that leads to true insight and understanding.

The purpose of faith is to lead humans out of the fatal poison of sin and ignorance towards certainty concerning God and to develop personal love and devotion for the Perfect and Living God. Faith guides human beings to fear God, shun sin, and progress morally and spiritually, culminating in the soul's nearness to God.

Faith is the path through which human beings transcend their base animalistic nature, rise through stages of moral and spiritual development, and ultimately devote their entire being to winning the true love and pleasure of their Creator. It is not merely intellectual assent but a transformative force that reforms natural inclinations and fosters divine attributes within the believer.

God endowed humans with the innate capacity and hunger for understanding and recognizing Him, as He fashioned the human soul with faculties that seek the eternal and perfect Truth. This capacity is analogous to the faculty of speech that defines a human's distinctiveness among creatures—just as speech is a gift from God, so too is faith a God-given faculty.

God wishes that His creatures recognize Him and derive benefit from His mercy, and faith is the means through which this recognition is realized. By investing human beings with this faculty, God ensures that we are not left in ignorance but are equipped to seek and achieve spiritual enlightenment.

Reason and faith are harmoniously intertwined. While reason can demonstrate the necessity of God's existence and guide understanding of the physical world, it falls short in confirming metaphysical truths and divine realities. Faith acts as the companion to reason, providing the certainty that reason alone cannot attain. But faith resting solely on tales, myths, or unsubstantiated stories is akin to idol worship and fails to guide one toward true salvation. Therefore, faith built on reason, divine signs, and spiritual experience is necessary in the understanding of True God and building a relationship with Him.

Faith is indispensable because without it, humans remain under the sway of sin and ignorance. Like one who unknowingly swallows poison, a person who lacks certainty of God's existence is prone to deliberate sin. Faith instills fear and love of God, which serve as powerful deterrents against sin. Moreover, faith strengthens the soul, providing spiritual nourishment akin to physical food, and empowers believers to endure hardships with patience and hope. It opens the path to divine grace, contentment, and true prosperity, both in this life and the hereafter.

A person with true faith experiences a transformation where moral vices are replaced by divine attributes such as courage, steadfastness, and love, and is freed from egotism and base desires. Conversely, lacking faith leads to spiritual blindness, moral decay, and ultimate ruin, as one remains disconnected from the Source of true life and sustenance.

In summary, faith is the vital bridge connecting human reason and divine truth, the seen and the unseen, the mortal and the eternal. It requires belief in the unseen, sincere devotion, and acceptance of God. Instilled by God as an innate faculty, faith serves the profound purpose of guiding humans to salvation, moral excellence, and ultimate happiness. Through faith, human beings gain certainty, overcome sin, and experience the living blessings of a relationship with the Perfect and Living God, which is the true paradise in this life and the hereafter.

Reflection:

In what ways do I currently understand the relationship between reason and faith, and how might I cultivate a faith that is both heartfelt and grounded in reason and experience?

Do I ascribe to blind faith that is based on stories and fiction instead of faith grounded in reason and facts?

Reaction:

Day 11-20: Find a quiet, secluded place at night and sit in a chair. Read the excerpt and reflect on the questions, supplicating before God for help and guidance. Avoid engaging in conversation afterwards.

Day 21: Justice

Reading:

Justice is a fundamental principle that governs both divine and human affairs, intricately linked to the concepts of reward and punishment. At its core, justice involves the fair and rightful allocation of consequences based on one's actions. Reward is bestowed upon the righteous, while punishment is meted out to the wrongdoers, thereby maintaining moral balance and social order. This principle is crucial not only for establishing order but also for fostering trust and righteousness among individuals.

In human interactions, exercising justice is indispensable. It ensures that the rights and dignity of each person are respected and that harm is neither inflicted unjustly nor overlooked. Justice upholds social harmony by encouraging individuals to act responsibly and with consideration toward others. Without justice, society would descend into chaos, marked by rampant wrongdoing, mistrust, and suffering. For example, if punishment were indiscriminately applied or withheld, the deterrent effect of justice would be lost, leading to increased transgressions and social disorder.

The human exercise of justice is inherently imperfect due to the influence of inferior faculties such as arrogance, greed, and the desire for power, which often override the universal principle of justice. These base tendencies lead individuals to commit various injustices, disregarding fairness and righteousness. The natural weakness of human nature means that people may fall short in upholding justice, succumbing to their passions and selfish desires. This imperfection is evident in the frequent moral failings and social disruptions caused by arrogance, pride, and envy. Therefore, it is crucial for individuals to constantly remind themselves of their own humility and to maintain a consciousness of the fear of God in all dealings. Recognizing that true justice and righteousness come from God, and that humans are fallible creatures accountable to a higher authority, helps to curb the misuse of faculties and guides one towards fairness and moral integrity in life's affairs.

Regarding God's exercise of justice, it is essential to recognize that God is the Sovereign Master, the Absolute Owner of all creation, Who bestows life, sustenance, and governance. Creatures, therefore, do not possess any right to demand justice from God. Instead, humans must acknowledge their utter dependence upon God and accept His judgments with humility. God's justice, unlike human justice, is perfect and operates inline with His boundless attributes and wisdom. Though He punishes sin, He also forgives abundantly, reflecting His mercy. God's justice and mercy are not contradictory but complementary, with mercy being the overarching attribute. Punishments serve as warnings and deterrents, and forgiveness arises from God's infinite compassion and understanding of human weakness. This nuanced relationship means that God's justice is not a mere infliction of penalty but a manifestation of His comprehensive governance that ultimately

leads to the spiritual growth and salvation of His servants.
In summary, justice is a divine and moral imperative that maintains the balance between reward and punishment, ensuring fairness in human conduct and divine governance. Its importance in human society cannot be overstated, as it preserves order and fosters trust. The integration of mercy and forgiveness within justice highlights the compassionate dimension necessary for a just society and spiritual life. Recognizing God's supreme justice and mercy with humility and faith allows humans to navigate their moral responsibilities while seeking divine favor and forgiveness.

Reflection:

In what ways do I recognize and accept the limitations of human justice compared to the perfect justice of God, and how does this awareness influence my trust in divine judgment and my pursuit of mercy and forgiveness?

Where is justice warranted and where is mercy and forgiveness warranted?

Reaction:

Day 21-30: Find a quiet, secluded place at night and sit on the floor in a kneeling position. Read the excerpt and reflect on the questions, supplicating before God for help and guidance. Try not to engage in conversation afterwards.

Day 22: Righteousness

Reading:

Righteousness, as viewed in the divine context, is a multifaceted concept that transcends mere outward behavior, embodying both a profound obedience to God and a sincere service to fellow human beings. It is not simply a set of rules to follow but a comprehensive moral and spiritual state of existence that is essential for true understanding of God and for building a lasting relationship with Him.

At its core, righteousness involves mindfulness of the Divine trusts and covenants, as well as all the trusts and covenants One has towards fellow human beings. It demands that a person forsake all forms of wrongdoing, such as adultery, theft, hypocrisy, arrogance, miserliness, and scorn for others. Beyond abstaining from evil, righteousness requires doing good.

Righteousness embodies two aspects: firstly, it is obedience to God, which means that a person's entire being, physical and spiritual faculties, is devoted to God alone, worshipping and loving Him without associating any partner. Secondly, it involves the service of God's creatures—sympathy, sharing their burdens and sorrows, and striving for their benefit purely for the sake of God.

While righteousness is not necessary for worldly learning, such as studies in grammar, physics, philosophy, astronomy, or medicine, it is indispensable for heavenly learning and the acquisition of spiritual knowledge. The understanding of divine mysteries and the true recognition of God require a righteous heart, free from arrogance and full of humility.

Righteousness serves as a gateway to heavenly knowledge because it aligns a person's inner state with the divine attributes, allowing them to receive spiritual insight. Without righteousness, a person might possess intellectual capacities but remain blind to true spiritual realities. True righteousness safeguards a person against extremes of doubt and skepticism, and opens the door to divine grace. It requires one to completely abandon major vices and gradually eradicate even the subtle and hidden moral defects such as jealousy, suspicion, arrogance, and pride. It requires one to exhibit politeness, generosity, forgiveness, patience, benevolence, sincerity, loyalty, and other noble qualities at the proper times and places, under the guidance of reason and understanding. It requires one to exercise God-given faculties—such as anger, forgiveness, and bravery—appropriately and in balance. It requires one to persist in righteous conduct, even in the face of trials and temptations, recognizing that human nature is prone to error and weakness, but that God's mercy and forgiveness are always available for the repentant. And it requires one to maintain humility and avoid arrogance, the highest form of vice and a serious barrier to righteousness.

True righteousness is marked by humility. A righteous person sees themselves as dependent upon God and acknowledges their own limitations. This humility is the seed from which faith and righteousness grow. Conversely, arrogance stems from excessive pride and self-esteem, which obscure spiritual insight and foster conflict and division among people

In summary, righteousness, in the divine perspective, is a holistic condition that encompasses both devotion to God and compassionate service to others. It is essential for the true understanding of God and the attainment of spiritual knowledge, serving as the foundation for a sincere and enduring relationship with the Divine. True righteousness requires a balanced exercise of all moral faculties, persistent humility, and an earnest effort to discard both overt and subtle vices. In contrast, arrogance stands as a formidable barrier to righteousness, alienating the heart from God and fellow human beings. The path of righteousness is thus a journey of moral refinement, spiritual awakening, and loving submission—leading ultimately to salvation and eternal bliss.

Reflection:

Which subtle moral defects such as arrogance, jealousy, or suspicion might I harbor, and how can I actively work to recognize and eradicate them from my character in order to become more righteous?

Am I only at the stage of avoiding evil or am I doing good as well in order to develop righteousness?

Reaction:

Day 21-30: Find a quiet, secluded place at night and sit on the floor in a kneeling position. Read the excerpt and reflect on the questions, supplicating before God for help and guidance. Try not to engage in conversation afterwards.

Day 23: Certainty

Reading:

Certainty is an essential concept that underpins true faith and guides human behavior towards righteousness. To have certainty about something means to possess an assured, unwavering conviction that transcends doubt and conjecture. It is the state where one moves beyond mere probability or conjecture based on stories, to a profound, personal belief that something indeed exists or is true.

Certainty is the firm conviction that a matter is true and real, not merely a possibility or a hypothesis. It is a belief so strong that it influences one's actions and decisions decisively. For example, no person consciously swallows poison or deliberately places their hand into a fire because they have certainty about the harm it will cause. This certainty is not based on hearsay but on clear understanding and experience. Similarly, certainty concerning the existence and attributes of God is foundational to adopting a faith that transforms a person's life.

The journey towards certainty regarding the unknown can be viewed as comprising three progressive stages: certainty by inference, certainty by sight, and certainty by experience. Certainty by inference is the initial stage where reason, observation, and reflection lead a person to conclude that something must exist or be true. For example, if one sees smoke, it is reasonable to conclude that there must be fire. Certainty by sight is the middle stage where reason's conjecture is confirmed through sight. For example, if someone sees flames, it is reasonable to conclude that there must be fire. Finally, certainty by experience is the final and highest stage that comes through personal, direct experience. For example, if one puts their hand into the fire, they know for certain that there is fire.

Certainty of God's existence is critical because it serves as the foundation of all moral and spiritual life. Without this certainty, a person lacks the motivation to fear God or shun sin. The absence of certainty about God can be likened to walking blindly, unaware of the dangers that lie ahead. For instance, people do not deliberately expose themselves to dangers like poison or wild animals because they have certainty about the harm involved. However, in the absence of certainty about God and the consequences of sin, many commit sins deliberately, as they do not perceive the true danger.

Certainty about God's existence and His justice instills a profound fear and love that deters one from sin. Just as a person with certainty about fire's danger would never thrust their hand into it, so too does the believer with certainty in God avoid sin because they know it brings punishment and spiritual ruin. This certainty is not mere intellectual agreement but a transformative conviction that changes one's inner disposition and behavior. It cultivates a personal love for God, which becomes the believer's paradise in this life and the hereafter.

In summary, certainty is not mere belief; it is a profound realization that shapes faith and moral conduct. It progresses from rational inference to confirmed observation and finally to personal experience. This journey is essential because only through certainty can one truly fear God, love Him, and shun sin. Thus, certainty concerning God is the cornerstone of salvation.

Reflection:

How can I move beyond mere belief or hearsay towards a deeper, personal certainty about the existence and attributes of God?

How does the analogy of avoiding physical danger (like fire or poison) because of certainty apply to my spiritual life and avoiding sin?

Reaction:

Day 21-30: Find a quiet, secluded place at night and sit on the floor in a kneeling position. Read the excerpt and reflect on the questions, supplicating before God for help and guidance. Try not to engage in conversation afterwards.

Day 24: Prayer

Reading:

Prayer, in its most profound sense, is the submission of one's humility and weakness to God, seeking fulfillment and aid from the Divine. It is not merely a ritualistic act but a heartfelt communication and a spiritual exercise that involves the whole being of a person. True prayer is marked by sincerity, faith, and a deep awareness of God's perfect attributes and power.

Prayer is the act through which a servant draws near to God, recognizing His greatness and their own helplessness. It is a demonstration of dependence upon the Creator and an acknowledgment that all power and beneficence lie with Him alone. Prayer is not just uttering words but involves a profound eagerness and humility, where the supplicant's heart is inspired by the greatness and mercy of God and the recognition of their own helplessness and need.

The nature of prayer is such that it requires the suspension of self-will and human faculties, allowing God's presence to take full control of the heart and soul. It is an act of surrender and devotion where the worshiper seeks to align their will with that of God. This spiritual submission is essential for prayer to become effective and transformative.

Prayer serves as a crucial link between the human and the Divine, fulfilling the soul's innate yearning for communion with God. It is a means through which humans acknowledge their limitations and seek divine guidance, support, and mercy. The purpose of prayer extends beyond mere requests; it nourishes the soul, strengthens spiritual faculties, and fosters a deep personal connection with God.

Moreover, prayer requires patience and steadfastness. It helps the believer to overcome the dominance of the ego and to develop sincerity and faithfulness. Through prayer, one's resolve is strengthened, and the heart is softened, opening the way to divine grace and spiritual enlightenment.

It is important to understand that God is self-sufficient and does not need human prayers. Rather, prayer is entirely for the benefit of the human being. God's mercy and grace envelop all creation, but through prayer, humans actively participate in their own spiritual development and draw nearer to God's bounties.

Prayer is a manifestation of a mutually attractive relationship between the servant and the Lord. While God's grace initially draws a person, it is through the person's sincere prayer and submission that this relationship deepens and bears fruit. Thus, prayer is a means of aligning oneself with divine will and fostering spiritual progress.

The acceptance of prayer depends on several conditions on the part of the human being including humility, sincerity, patience, steadfastness, alignment with the divine will, and avoidance of improper requests. But first and foremost, a believer must understand that acceptance of prayer is purely due to the grace of

God, for He is the Lord and has no obligation towards the supplicant. God's greatness and mercy, combined with human helplessness, create the spiritual atmosphere that nourishes true prayer. Without this humility, prayer becomes empty words or mere formality lacking spiritual power.

Prayer has profound effects on the supplicant's life and spiritual state. It attracts divine attention, strengthens the faith, improves certainty of belief, and results in signs for the believer that provide comfort for the soul.

In summary, prayer is a sacred and powerful means through which human beings acknowledge their dependence on God, seek His mercy, and cultivate a deep, personal relationship with the Divine. It requires humility, sincerity, and steadfastness, and its effects transform the heart, strengthen faith, and draw down divine blessings. God does not depend on our prayers; rather we depend on them to seek his grace and mercy. Prayer is essential for our spiritual well-being and progress, serving as a means to increase our certainty of faith in God and bring about improvement in our life.

Reflection:

Do I believe in the power of prayer?

How patient and steadfast am I in my prayer, especially when my supplications seem unanswered, and do I trust that acceptance depends solely on God's grace and wisdom?

Do I understand that prayer is not for God's benefit but for my own spiritual nourishment and progress, and how can this awareness deepen my relationship with the Divine?

Reaction:

Day 21-30: Find a quiet, secluded place at night and sit on the floor in a kneeling position. Read the excerpt and reflect on the questions, supplicating before God for help and guidance. Try not to engage in conversation afterwards.

Day 25: Repentance

Reading:

Human beings, by their very nature, are frail and prone to error. This inherent weakness, combined with the weight of countless divine commandments, makes it inevitable that individuals will fall short in their obedience to God. Recognizing this reality, the concept of repentance holds a central place in the spiritual journey of a believer, offering a pathway to forgiveness and eventual deliverance.

Human beings are endowed with responsibilities that are lofty and demanding. Yet, their nature is imperfect, susceptible to desires and inclinations that often lead them astray. As a result, it is natural and expected that they would fail to uphold all divine commandments perfectly. This shortcoming is not merely an unfortunate flaw but part of the human condition that necessitates the act of repentance. It is through sincere repentance that a person acknowledges his/her faults and seeks to return to the path of righteousness. Without this mechanism, the spiritual downfall would be irreversible.

If God were not the Acceptor of repentance, the entire human enterprise would be doomed. The acceptance of repentance by God is a source of hope and a cornerstone of divine mercy. It is precisely because God turns towards those who repent that humanity can endure and aspire to moral and spiritual growth. The acknowledgment of human frailty and the availability of forgiveness prevent despair and encourage continuous striving towards virtue.

To reject repentance and forgiveness is, in essence, to close the door on human progress. Without the possibility of being forgiven, individuals would be trapped in a cycle of guilt and despair, incapable of transformation. The eternal law of God does not demand an impossible standard of flawless behavior but rather sets forth a merciful system where stumbling is expected, and the crucial factor is the genuine return to God through sincere repentance. This divine mercy is not a one-time concession but an everlasting attribute, where God continuously turns to those who sincerely seek Him despite their faults.

True repentance is not merely a verbal declaration or a momentary feeling of regret. It involves several critical conditions including genuine remorse, abandonment of evil thoughts and actions, and firm resolve. These conditions ensure that repentance is not superficial but a transformative act that reorients a person's life towards God. When these conditions are met, repentance acts as a spiritual cleanser that wipes away the stain of sin. This purification is not symbolic but real, restoring the individual to a state of moral and spiritual health. Continual repentance and seeking forgiveness also cultivate humility, washing out arrogance and pride, which are barriers to true spiritual progress.

The relationship between repentance and deliverance is profound. Deliverance, understood as salvation and eternal prosperity, is achievable only when a person turns away from sin and returns to God with sincerity. Repentance is the prerequisite for this deliverance because it reconnects the soul with divine mercy and opens the doors to spiritual growth. It is through repentance that a person moves from the darkness of sin to the light of virtue. The requirements for deliverance thus encompass not only belief and understanding but also the practical act of turning away from wrongdoing and sincerely seeking God's forgiveness.

In summary, repentance is an essential and merciful provision for humankind's inherent frailty. It is a divine gift that sustains human hope and progress. The acceptance of sincere repentance by God underscores His boundless mercy and compassion, ensuring that no soul is lost beyond redemption. By fulfilling the conditions of true repentance, believers can cleanse themselves of sin, restore their relationship with the Creator, and embark on the path to ultimate deliverance and spiritual fulfillment.

Reflection:

Is there a grave wrong I've committed that I want to seek repentance for from God?

How does understanding God's role as the Acceptor of repentance influence my hope and motivation for continuous moral and spiritual growth?

Reaction:

Day 21-30: Find a quiet, secluded place at night and sit on the floor in a kneeling position. Read the excerpt and reflect on the questions, supplicating before God for help and guidance. Try not to engage in conversation afterwards.

Day 26: Forgiveness

Reading:

Forgiveness, often regarded as a noble and virtuous quality, holds a profound place in both human ethics and divine attributes. It is generally understood as the act of pardoning someone for a wrong or offense committed against us. However, forgiveness, while inherently good, is not an unqualified virtue; it requires discernment in its exercise, and it must be practiced at the proper time and occasion.

While forgiveness is praised as a high moral quality, it is important to recognize that exercising forgiveness indiscriminately or at all times can be harmful. Human nature, bestowed with a variety of faculties, includes both the capacity for forgiveness and for justified indignation or retribution. The balance between these faculties is governed by reason, which acts as a just ruler guiding their appropriate use. For instance, forgiveness and meekness are beneficial when applied on the proper occasion, leading to material and spiritual benefit for both the forgiver and the forgiven. However, if forgiveness is extended indiscriminately and on every occasion, it can encourage offenders to persist in wrongdoing and cause greater harm. This misuse of forgiveness can disrupt social order and is ultimately detrimental to both individuals and society.

The forgiveness of God is fundamentally different in its nature and operation from human forgiveness. God's forgiveness is an eternal and inherent attribute, reflecting His mercy and compassion towards His creation. His forgiveness is supreme and surpasses other divine attributes such as justice, because He is the Lord and Master over all things and not bound by any law of justice. Unlike human forgiveness, which can be limited by emotional capacity, reason, or circumstance, God's forgiveness is boundless and ever available to those who sincerely seek it through repentance. That is, God's forgiveness is not contingent on human perfection; rather, it is extended even to sinners who turn to Him with true remorse and resolve to reform. But since God knows the innermost intentions of the heart, He knows whether a person's repentance is sincere and genuine or merely superficial and fake.

God has also instilled the noble attribute of forgiveness within human beings, encouraging us to practice forgiveness towards one another. Though we are inherently imperfect, God desires that we emulate His mercy by exercising forgiveness at the appropriate times and occasions. This is how we can foster harmony and peaceful coexistence among people. By learning to manifest forgiveness in its proper degree and context, we align ourselves with divine wisdom and contribute to a society grounded in compassion and justice.

In summary, forgiveness is a vital moral quality that fosters harmony and personal growth, but it must be exercised with wisdom and balance, recognizing that unlimited forgiveness can be detrimental. Human forgiveness, while valuable, is limited and imperfect, whereas God's forgiveness is infinite and boundless, accessible through sincere repentance. Understanding this divine attribute encourages humans to seek God's mercy, strive for moral reform, and cultivate forgiveness as a balanced and reasoned virtue in our own lives.

Reflection:

Do I understand the difference between human forgiveness and divine forgiveness?

Do I understand that indiscriminate forgiveness can sometimes lead to harm and instead, it has to be practiced at the right time and place?

Reaction:

Day 21-30: Find a quiet, secluded place at night and sit on the floor in a kneeling position. Read the excerpt and reflect on the questions, supplicating before God for help and guidance. Try not to engage in conversation afterwards.

Day 27: Peace

Reading:

Peace is a concept that transcends mere absence of conflict; it is a profound state of harmony, balance, and well-being that begins within the individual and radiates outward to families and societies. To understand peace fully, one must explore its definition, its various levels, and the means by which it can be attained, as well as the complex role of violence when it is employed with the intention of restoring peace. Equally important is the notion of returning to the Creator in a state of peace, which marks the culmination of a peaceful life.

Peace, in its truest sense, is a state of inner tranquility and moral integrity that governs one's soul and behavior. It is not simply the absence of turmoil but the presence of righteousness, humility, and love within the heart. Peace encompasses the harmonious exercise of natural faculties—such as forgiveness, forbearance, bravery, generosity, and sincerity—tempered by reason and exercised at their proper times and places.

Peace manifests on multiple levels, each interrelated and essential for the establishment of peace in all aspects of life. Inner peace is the foundation of all other kinds of peace. It refers to the calmness and contentment of the soul, the control of passions, the surrender of ego, and the establishment of a sincere relationship with God. Inner peace arises from righteousness, faith, and the love of the Divine. It is marked by the absence of spiritual torment and the presence of contentment and delight in worship and remembrance of God. Inner peace is not passively acquired but must be actively sought through spiritual exercise such as seeking forgiveness and repentance. These acts serve as the antidote to sin and spiritual ailments, cleansing the soul and enabling progress towards moral and spiritual perfection.

Peace in one's surroundings starts at home. It is nurtured through mutual respect, compassion, courteous behavior, sincerity, and the fulfillment of trusts and covenants among family members. Relationships between a husband and wife and between parents and children need to follow the natural laws instituted by God in order to attain peace in the household. Each member of the household has a natural role to play in the family unit that differs from everyone else and unless these roles are nurtured and respected, peace in the household cannot be maintained.

Finally, social peace builds on the foundation of justice, righteousness, and cooperation among people based on laws. It involves the orderly cooperation of nations, the rule of law, and the prevention of chaos that would arise from conflicting interests and hostilities among multiple powers.

While peace is the ultimate goal, history and human experience show that violence may sometimes be undertaken with the intention of restoring or establishing peace. This must be approached with great caution and moral discernment. Violence for its own sake is condemned, but when employed as a means to uphold justice, protect the innocent, and maintain social order, it can be considered a necessary evil that serves the greater good of peace.

The ultimate peace is the peace of the soul at death. It is vital that one returns to the Creator in a state of spiritual peace—having purified the soul through repentance, sincere worship, and righteous living. This can only be achieved if one lives their life in accordance with the dictates of God and keeping in mind the fact that one day, death will overtake us and we will need to return to our Creator and give an account of our actions.

In summary, peace is a multi-dimensional reality starting from the inner self and extending to family, society, and the world at large. It is achieved through faith, moral rectitude, sincere devotion, and the balanced exercise of human faculties under the guidance of reason and divine revelation. While violence may sometimes be necessary to uphold peace, it must always be governed by justice and aimed at restoring harmony. Ultimately, true peace culminates in a soul that returns to the Creator reconciled, humble, and filled with divine love—a state that embodies the highest aspiration of human existence.

Reflection:

How can I cultivate and maintain inner peace in my daily life, especially through spiritual practices such as seeking forgiveness, repentance, and sincere worship?

How do I understand the balance between the rejection of violence and the moral discernment required when violence is used as a means to restore justice and peace?

Am I living my life in a way that prepares my soul for ultimate peace at death?

Reaction:

Day 21-30: Find a quiet, secluded place at night and sit on the floor in a kneeling position. Read the excerpt and reflect on the questions, supplicating before God for help and guidance. Try not to engage in conversation afterwards.

Day 28: Kindness & Sympathy

Reading:

Kindness and sympathy are fundamental moral qualities that form the fabric of human goodness and social harmony. They encompass the natural inclination to do good to others, to alleviate suffering, and to foster benevolence in interpersonal relationships. When exercised properly, these qualities elevate both the giver and the receiver to higher moral and spiritual states.

The practical manifestation of kindness and sympathy is service to humanity. When a person acts kindly, whether by offering help, alleviating hardship, or sharing in others' sorrows, they fulfill the divine trust and covenants bestowed upon them. This service is not limited to physical aid but extends to emotional and spiritual support, sharing burdens, and fostering fellowship among people.

Service to others motivated by kindness and sympathy is a form of devotion to God, reflecting one's love and obedience to the Creator through compassion for His creatures. Such service requires a readiness to endure hardships and to sacrifice personal convenience for the welfare of others, embodying the essence of true worship.

Kindness and sympathy can be described as specific forms of a broader concept of doing good. Doing goodness can be categorized in three stages: 1) doing good in return for good, 2) taking initiative in doing good, and 3) spontaneous goodness.

The first stage of doing good in return for good is the most basic level of kindness, where a person reciprocates kindness received. Even an average individual can attain this stage by responding benevolently to those who do good to them. It is a natural human response and an initial step towards moral excellence.

In the second stage, a person extends kindness proactively to those who may not have a claim on it. This form of benevolence is more difficult because it requires acting without immediate benefit or expectation of gratitude. However, it may still contain an unconscious desire for acknowledgment, and the benefactor may feel aggrieved if their kindness is met with ingratitude.

The third and highest stage can be likened to the kindness that a mother has for her child; a kindness that is characterized by spontaneous, unconditional goodness, regardless of the response. This pure form of kindness arises naturally and is an expression of profound love and selflessness and cannot be surpassed.

Kindness and sympathy, when exercised at their highest levels, contribute to the purification of the human soul. They are means through which a person cultivates true fidelity, sincerity towards God, and genuine concern for fellow beings. These virtues help in discarding evil and promoting good, fostering social harmony and personal spiritual growth. It calls for humility, patience, and forgiveness, balanced with justice and rightful indignation when needed.

In summary, kindness and sympathy are not only natural faculties but are elevated to moral and spiritual virtues through reason, reflection, and divine guidance. They manifest in service to humanity, reflecting true devotion to God. Progressively, one moves from reciprocating good, to initiating kindness without entitlement, to spontaneous and unconditional goodness akin to a mother's love. Cultivating these qualities is essential for personal moral reformation and achieving the true purpose of human life—worship and love of God through service to His creation.

Reflection:

At which stage of doing good do I currently find myself: reciprocating kindness, proactively initiating kindness, or offering spontaneous and unconditional goodness?

How can cultivating kindness and sympathy contribute to the purification of my soul and my relationship with God and fellow human beings?

Reaction:

Day 21-30: Find a quiet, secluded place at night and sit on the floor in a kneeling position. Read the excerpt and reflect on the questions, supplicating before God for help and guidance. Try not to engage in conversation afterwards.

Day 29: Sacrifice

Reading:

Sacrifice is a concept deeply ingrained in the natural order and spiritual teachings alike. Observing the law of nature reveals a consistent principle: the inferior is always sacrificed to safeguard the superior. This principle manifests across all facets of creation—from the microscopic germs to the vast animal kingdom—all sacrificed for the preservation and well-being of human beings. It is never the case that a superior entity is sacrificed for the inferior, and anyone who proposes such an idea contradicts the fundamental law of nature.

This natural law offers a profound lesson for human conduct, particularly regarding our relationship with physical possessions, wealth, and life itself. Physical possessions and money, while valuable, are inherently inferior to human life. Recognizing this hierarchy, it is natural and justified that money and possessions be sacrificed for the betterment and preservation of human life. In everyday life, we practice this principle on a limited scale: we willingly spend money on ourselves and our families to ensure their health, comfort, and survival. However, spiritual enlightenment calls for a broader application of this sacrifice—spending wealth for the benefit of all humanity. This higher form of sacrifice demands that we overcome greed and fully realize that the Bestower of all wealth and possessions is God. It is by His grace that we have been entrusted with these resources, and He desires that we use them to aid those segments of His creation less fortunate than ourselves.

The essence of spending in the way of others lies in understanding the divine wisdom behind human diversity. God, in His infinite wisdom, has created a diverse human society where individuals are bestowed with differing capacities and circumstances. This diversity is part of the grand design for the progress of life as a whole. Consequently, not everyone is fortunate enough to receive the same material blessings or opportunities that some others have been granted. Recognizing that whatever we possess is ultimately a blessing from God, it becomes incumbent upon us to share a portion of these blessings with those who are less fortunate, whether financially or otherwise. This act of sacrifice is both a responsibility and an expression of gratitude toward the Creator.

Such sacrifice is not merely a social duty but a spiritual one, reflecting a deeper realization of the unity and interdependence ordained by God. By willingly giving up part of our wealth for the welfare of others, we acknowledge God's sovereignty over all creation and manifest our sincere devotion and love for Him. This sacrifice transcends mere charity; it is a means through which divine attributes such as mercy, compassion, and generosity are cultivated within us, bringing us closer to God and aligning our lives with His eternal law. This is the essence of spending in the way of God.

In summary, sacrifice, as observed in the law of nature, teaches us the prioritization of the superior over the inferior, a principle that must be reflected in our lives through the willing sacrifice of wealth and possessions for the betterment of humanity. This sacrifice is grounded in the recognition that all we have is bestowed by God and that sharing with those less fortunate is both a moral and spiritual imperative. Through such selfless giving, we not only uphold the natural law but also grow in spiritual enlightenment and closeness to God.

Reflection:

In what ways can I cultivate a deeper awareness that all my blessings are ultimately from God, and how does this realization impact my willingness to share with those less fortunate?

Do I view acts of giving and sacrifice merely as social duties, or do I see them as spiritual practices that bring me closer to God and develop divine attributes like mercy and compassion within me?

Reaction:

Day 21-30: Find a quiet, secluded place at night and sit on the floor in a kneeling position. Read the excerpt and reflect on the questions, supplicating before God for help and guidance. Try not to engage in conversation afterwards.

Day 30: Miracles

Reading:

The concept of miracles has often been misunderstood and misrepresented by many across various cultures and religious traditions. At its core, a miracle is a manifestation of God's power that transcends human capability and defies ordinary imagination. It is not some fantastical tale or a psychic phenomenon but a profound sign from the Divine, affirming the truth of a holy person and the unity of God.

Throughout history, followers of various religions have ascribed fantastical stories to their prophets and founders. These stories often include exaggerated or impossible feats that stray from the fundamental doctrine of the oneness and perfection of God. Such tales, rooted in superstition or embellishment, contradict the true unity of God by implying the existence of God-like powers or associating God with lesser beings.

Contrary to popular belief, miracles are not necessarily violations of natural laws. Indeed, the most impressive and profound miracles often occur within the confines of God's established law of nature. These manifestations do not contradict the divine attributes of unity, holiness, or perfection but rather highlight them. God's acts always align with His eternal attributes and laws, and what might appear extraordinary to human beings is in fact a natural extension of divine will operating through means that may be beyond human understanding.

One remarkable example is the spiritual transformation brought about by holy persons among their followers. Such a transformation—marked by moral reform, steadfast faith, and inner enlightenment—is itself a miracle, especially when we reflect on the difficulty of changing one's long-held beliefs and practices.

A common form of miracle attributed to holy personages is the foretelling of future events. This phenomenon often baffles skeptics who consider it a breach of natural law. However, such knowledge is imparted by God revealing hidden matters to those sincere servants who are spiritually prepared. This revelation is not contrary to nature but a supernatural assistance bestowed upon the recipient, akin to the unseen forces working through angels or spiritual intermediaries.

Prayer occupies a central role in the manifestation of miracles. When a supplicant approaches God with perfect certainty, sincerity, and steadfastness, their prayers can invoke divine assistance that influences the elements and heavenly bodies. For instance, prayers can bring about rain or alleviate famine, with angels guiding clouds and regulating natural phenomena according to God's command. The efficacy of prayer is tied directly to the supplicant's faith and persistence, reflecting a dynamic relationship between human effort and divine action.

The essence of a true miracle is that it is extraordinary yet fully consistent with God's attributes of Unity, Holiness, and Perfection. Miracles serve as signs that establish the truth of a holy person and affirm the Oneness and Supreme Power of God. They are not arbitrary breaches of natural law but are integrated within the perfect order of the universe, revealing the living presence and active governance of God in the world. That is not to say that God cannot violate the laws of nature. Indeed, He can do whatever He wills. But the beauty of His perfect system is that he exhibits miracles within the scope of the law of nature that He has chosen to put in place.

In summary, miracles should not be reduced to mere stories or spectacles. They are profound manifestations of divine power that invite reflection, strengthen faith, and confirm the authenticity of God's Messengers. Whether through the spiritual transformation of individuals, the revelation of hidden knowledge, or the response to prayer influencing natural phenomena, miracles stand as enduring testimonies to the living and perfect God Who governs all creation.

Reflection:

Am I able to distinguish between fanciful stories about miracles and the true purpose of miracles as signs affirming the authenticity of God's Messengers and the living presence of God?

Are there any miracles that have happened in my own life that help to affirm my faith in the existence of God?

Reaction:

Day 21-30: Find a quiet, secluded place at night and sit on the floor in a kneeling position. Read the excerpt and reflect on the questions, supplicating before God for help and guidance. Try not to engage in conversation afterwards.

Day 31: Worship

Reading:

Worship, at its essence, is the profound expression of humility by the creation in recognition of the greatness and perfection of The Creator. It is the natural outcome of a being acknowledging its own limitations and impermanence in contrast to the absolute majesty, power, and perfection of God. This humility is not merely a passive acknowledgment but an active devotion, surrender, and love directed towards God, Who is the fountainhead of all existence and salvation.

Every element of the universe, from the smallest atom to the vast expanse of the cosmos, in its own way, worships God. This worship is manifested through the continuous and unwavering performance of their intended functions. The sun rises and sets, providing light and heat; the moon follows its orbit; rivers flow; seeds sprout and grow—all in accordance with the decrees of The Creator. This perpetual order and harmony testify to a greater presence governing all things. These natural phenomena, being bound by the laws and limits set by God, are in constant submission to Him, thereby "worshiping" through their obedience and unceasing activity.

Human beings, as the pinnacle of creation, possess a unique capacity that distinguishes them from all other creatures—the faculty of free will. Unlike other forms of creation, which are inherently programmed to fulfill their purpose, humans have the autonomy to choose their paths. This capacity allows humans to engage in the highest form of worship: conscious, intentional devotion to God. However, with this autonomy comes great responsibility. Humans must recognize their ultimate purpose and pursue it sincerely. This purpose is not self-determined but is ordained by The Creator, as with every other creation. While humans can imagine and pursue many purposes, the true and ultimate purpose is to worship God. This worship is not a burdensome obligation; rather it is for our own benefit and is the fulfillment of the very reason of our existence. It is through this worship that humans align with the divine order and attain true meaning in life.

The unique gift of free will elevates human beings to a distinguished place within creation, but it also imposes a duty to seek and recognize the True God. Unlike other creatures whose worship is involuntary and automatic, humans must actively embark on the journey of faith—beginning with the understanding of God's perfect existence and attributes and culminating in a deep personal relationship with Him through worship. Failure to do so results in wasting one's life and missing the ultimate purpose of our existence.

It is vital to understand that God does not require human worship for His own benefit. He is self-sufficient, free from any need or deficiency. Rather, worship is for the benefit of humankind itself. Individually, worship provides inner peace, spiritual fulfillment, and the true and complete experience of life.

Collectively, it establishes the foundation for a harmonious and peaceful society, which is essential for the survival and flourishing of the human race. Worship cultivates righteousness, justice, and compassion, facilitating coexistence and mutual respect among people.

In summary, worship is the natural and necessary response of humility of the creation to the greatness of the Creator. It is evident throughout the universe, from the orderly motions of celestial bodies to the intricate workings of the smallest particles. Human beings, endowed with free will, have the unique capacity to consciously worship God, which constitutes their ultimate purpose. This purpose, like that of all creation, is divinely ordained, not self-imposed. The exercise of free will entails the responsibility to recognize the True God and devote oneself to Him through worship. God does not need or desire to be worshipped. Rather, worship of God is a source of profound benefit for humanity, bringing individual peace and societal harmony.

Reflection:

How does recognizing that worship benefits me personally and society as a whole change my view about my purpose in life?

Am I taking the time out of my daily routine to worship God?

Reaction:

Day 31-40: Wake up in the middle of the night and find a quiet, secluded place to sit on the floor in a kneeling position. Read the excerpt and reflect on the questions, supplicating before God for help and guidance. Go back to sleep without engaging in conversation with anyone.

Day 32: Destiny

Reading:

The concept of destiny and predestination has long been a subject of much confusion. At its core, there is no question that everything in existence operates under the command of God—He is the Creator, Sustainer, and Controller of all things. From the vast universe to the smallest particles, all function within His perfect design and wisdom. In light of this clear divine sovereignty, many grapple with what destiny truly means, especially regarding human free will and responsibility.

Destiny is a complex and often misunderstood concept. Some people, especially atheists, argue that if God controls everything, then human effort is meaningless; that whatever happens is simply "destined" and we bear no responsibility for our actions. This misunderstanding can lead to a nihilistic or fatalistic outlook on life, where one might blame God for every misfortune or failure, thereby living a life devoid of purpose or accountability. Such a view is incorrect and contrary to the balanced teachings of God. Destiny is not an unyielding chain that negates human effort; rather, it is a grand design that includes both divine decree and human choice.

To clarify this, it is essential to differentiate between two types of destiny: absolute decree and suspended decree. Absolute decree refers to divine determinations that cannot be altered by any means. These are fixed by God and inevitably come to pass. Suspended decree, on the other hand, depends on human action and prayer. These decrees can be changed or averted within the framework of God's law. An illustrative example of absolute decree is death. No matter the advances in medicine or technology, every human being will ultimately face death; this is predetermined and unalterable. Yet, within this absolute decree is room for suspended decree: one may hasten death through unhealthy living or unsafe actions, or in extreme cases, committing suicide.

Another simpler example is that of throwing an object into the air. According to the laws of nature, it is destined to fall back down and hit the ground. However, depending on your actions, you can choose to catch the object, thereby preventing it from hitting the ground. It would be wrong to claim "it was destined that I caught the ball" as if you had no role in that action. You made a conscious decision and exerted effort within God's laws to intervene in the ball's fall. This example, though seemingly trivial, highlights a profound truth: we are responsible for our actions and their consequences and cannot blame God for negative outcomes resulting from our choices.

A frequent objection is that if God already knows the past, present, and future, then how can human actions genuinely affect the future? The key to understanding this lies in recognizing that God is beyond time. He is the Creator of time and perceives all moments—past, present, and future—simultaneously, as if laid out before Him. Our perception of the future as "unknown" is limited by our temporal existence and the laws of nature that God has established. Hence, while God's knowledge is perfect and complete, human beings operate within temporal constraints and possess genuine free will to make choices and affect our future.

God's fundamental attributes are rooted in grace and mercy, love and benevolence. He is the source of all good and wishes the welfare of His creatures. Negative consequences result not from God's compulsion but from human actions that deviate from the good. God does not force us to act against our will within the laws of nature; rather, destiny incorporates universal laws alongside human choice and sincere supplication. It is like a grand river flowing inevitably toward its destination (absolute decrees), yet within its currents are smaller streams (suspended decrees) whose paths can be influenced by obstacles or human intervention. We cannot change the flow of the river, but we can choose to go down different routes—all of which lead to death and returning back to our Creator.

In relation to our purpose in life, God has created this world and humanity for a purpose—that purpose is an absolute decree that will be fulfilled. However, the suspended decree within this grand design concerns the role each individual plays. Will we be contributors to God's plan by following His guidance and striving for good? Or will we be indifferent, or worse, oppositional? Our choices determine our value and standing in God's sight. This dynamic interplay between divine decree and human responsibility underscores the meaningfulness of our lives and actions.

In summary, the concept of destiny and predestination encompasses both the absolute and the suspended decrees of God. While everything operates under God's supreme command, not all events are fixed in such a way that human effort is meaningless. Absolute decrees, such as death, are certain and unchangeable, yet within those decrees, suspended decrees allow for human choice, effort, and prayer to influence outcomes. God's knowledge transcends time, and His benevolent attributes ensure that destiny is part of a wise and purposeful design. Ultimately, humans bear responsibility for their choices and must engage actively and sincerely in their lives, contributing positively to the divine plan.

Reflection:

How do I understand the balance between God's absolute decree and my own free will in my daily life?

How does recognizing God's perfect knowledge beyond time affect my perspective on my responsibility and accountability for my actions?

Reaction:

Day 31-40: Wake up in the middle of the night and find a quiet, secluded place to sit on the floor in a kneeling position. Read the excerpt and reflect on the questions, supplicating before God for help and guidance. Go back to sleep without engaging in conversation with anyone.

Day 33: Suffering

Reading:

The question of suffering is one that has perplexed humanity across ages and cultures. Many wonder: If God is merciful and compassionate, why does pain and suffering persist in the world? This inquiry is not merely philosophical but deeply personal, touching the lives of individuals who experience hardship. To understand suffering in a comprehensive manner, it is essential to explore its nature, purpose, and place within the divine order.

At the most fundamental level, suffering is the antithesis of pleasure and ease. Just as light cannot be comprehended without darkness, pleasure cannot be fully appreciated without pain or suffering. This duality is intrinsic to the human experience. We cannot grasp the concept of comfort without having encountered discomfort. Similarly, suffering defines and gives meaning to joy and relief. This interplay is a natural part of existence and provides context for the spectrum of human emotions and experiences.

Suffering also functions as a necessary consequence under the divine law of nature. Every action initiated by an individual results in a reaction governed by God's eternal law. For example, swallowing poison leads inevitably to death—a clear manifestation of this natural law. The reaction of death is not arbitrary but a necessary and ordained consequence of the action taken. Analogously, when a person acts carelessly or contrary to divine guidance, suffering follows as a natural outcome of those actions. Thus, suffering is not a punishment arbitrarily imposed but a result of the inherent laws that govern the universe and human conduct.

Suffering in the form of trials and difficulties that befall a believer, especially in the interval between supplication and the acceptance of prayer, serves a higher divine purpose. These challenges strengthen resolve, build courage, and cultivate moral qualities such as patience and steadfastness. The experience of suffering teaches endurance and humility, enabling individuals to develop virtues that define true humanity.

Suffering is instrumental in moral development. Human beings possess a range of faculties—physical, mental, and spiritual—and the exercise of these faculties often occurs through the experience of hardship. For instance, the quality of patience is not merely a passive endurance but an active moral virtue that strengthens character. Similarly, forgiveness, compassion, and empathy can be deepened through personal experience of pain. Without suffering, these moral qualities would remain dormant or underdeveloped. Hence, suffering is a crucible in which the human soul is refined and elevated.

Suffering is intertwined with the very fabric of life; it cannot be understood in isolation. Just as a shadow is a byproduct of light, suffering is inseparable from the experience of growth and existence. Our collective human history demonstrates that suffering has often been the catalyst for progress. Many scientific discoveries and technological inventions arose from the urgent need to alleviate pain and discomfort. The relentless quest to understand disease, improve health, and enhance well-being is motivated by the universal experience of suffering. Thus, suffering propels civilization forward and fosters innovation and knowledge.

The experience of suffering is not limited to human morality or personal trials but extends to the natural world and the process of life itself. Diseases, congenital defects, and physical deformities—often sources of suffering—are integral to the evolutionary process. Diversity within species, including imperfections, drives evolution by natural selection. Without such diversity, life would stagnate and ultimately cease to exist.

The question of suffering experienced by children, such as those with congenital defects, must also be addressed. It is important to view this within the broader framework of life's evolutionary and divine design. The presence of disease and suffering at all levels of life—from microorganisms to humans—is part of the natural order that fosters growth, adaptation, and survival. While painful and distressing, these phenomena are not without purpose; they contribute to the continuous process by which life evolves and improves over generations. So while in our limited view, the suffering of a child may seem unjust, in the large scheme of life, it is a byproduct of the evolutionary process.

In summary, suffering, while often painful and perplexing, is a necessary and meaningful aspect of life under divine providence. It complements pleasure by giving it context and significance; it operates as a natural consequence of human actions under the eternal laws set by God. Far from being mere punishment, suffering is a test that cultivates patience, courage, and moral growth. It is inseparable from the human experience and serves as a catalyst for personal development and societal progress. Moreover, suffering is deeply embedded in the natural evolutionary process, driving the diversity and advancement of life. Understanding suffering in this holistic way allows believers to embrace it with patience and faith, recognizing it as part of a divine plan aimed at ultimate perfection and salvation.

Reflection:

In what ways can I view the suffering and trials I face as opportunities for moral growth, such as developing patience, courage, and empathy?

How might recognizing suffering as a natural consequence under divine law influence my response to difficulties and my sense of personal responsibility?

Reaction:

Day 31-40: Wake up in the middle of the night and find a quiet, secluded place to sit on the floor in a kneeling position. Read the excerpt and reflect on the questions, supplicating before God for help and guidance. Go back to sleep without engaging in conversation with anyone.

Day 34: Morality

Reading:

Morality, in the most general terms, can be understood as the proper use of human faculties at the right time and in the right measure, regulated by reason and aligned with the eternal attributes of God. It is not a subjective or relative concept shaped by fluctuating human opinions or circumstances but is rooted in divine principles that transcend time and culture.

The proper exercise of human faculties—such as bravery, forgiveness, humility, anger—in a manner that is appropriate to the occasion and measured by wisdom and discernment and aligned with the will of God leads to moral behavior. A human faculty becomes truly moral only when used under the guidance of reason, at the proper time, and in the proper measure. For example, qualities like bravery, generosity, forgiveness, and even anger are natural faculties endowed to humans. When these faculties are exercised judiciously, they become moral virtues. However, if misapplied or used excessively, they can turn harmful or immoral.

Morality is not merely an arbitrary code defined by human societies but is objective and grounded in the attributes of God. Human beings cannot redefine what is moral based on personal whims or the changing values of the times. Instead, true morality corresponds to God's perfect attributes such as justice, mercy, wisdom, and benevolence, which serve as an immutable standard for human conduct.

Morals are deeply rooted in human being's natural states and faculties. These faculties are reflections or manifestations of divine qualities implanted within human nature by God. For instance, the faculty of envy, often deemed negative, is not inherently evil. Envy becomes bad when it manifests as coveting material wealth or status at the expense of others. However, when envy motivates a person towards excelling in righteousness and attaining closeness to God—as seen in the saints—it is transformed into a positive quality and a spiritual incentive.

Similarly, natural qualities such as tenderness, bravery, mercy, forgiveness, generosity, and peacefulness correspond to inner moral states when exercised with reason and at the right time. These natural states, when regulated by reason and moral consciousness, become true moral qualities. For example, a child's natural aversion to taking another's property is the root of honesty and integrity, but it requires conscious application and understanding to mature into a moral virtue.

Morality can be broadly divided into two categories. The first comprises those moral qualities that enable a person to discard evil—avoiding harm to others in terms of life, property, honor, or reputation. The second category includes those that empower a person to do good—benefiting others through kind words, helpful deeds, protection, and forgiveness even when harm has been done. For example, overlooking a justified punishment or choosing forgiveness over retaliation falls within the domain of doing good and reflects high moral conduct.

Moral reform is possible and achievable through sincere effort, dedication, and particularly through repentance and seeking forgiveness. These acts are crucial because human nature is imperfect, prone to error, and influenced by passions and ego. Repentance involves rejecting evil thoughts and actions, feeling genuine remorse, and resolving firmly not to revert to previous vices. Seeking forgiveness acts as spiritual exercise, strengthening the soul and enabling moral progress.

Moral values are not static; they can develop and mature within a person who strives sincerely and consistently. Even those who fall into sin can reform morally by turning to God with a sincere heart, given that God is inherently forgiving and merciful. This dynamic process shows that morality is not an unattainable ideal but an evolving state that depends on human will and divine grace.

Truthfulness is a fundamental enabler of morality. It is a natural human disposition to dislike falsehood; however, true morality requires that a person remains truthful even when it is challenging or risky to do so. Telling the truth only when safe or convenient does not constitute genuine moral integrity. The true test of moral character requires sticking to the truth consistently, especially when facing loss or harm.

In summary, morality is the proper use of human faculties, exercised at the right time and in the right measure under the guidance of reason, and aligned with the eternal attributes of God. It is objective, rooted in divine qualities manifested within human nature, and not something that we as humans can subjectively decide based on our preferences or circumstances. Moral reform and development are possible through sincere effort, repentance, and seeking forgiveness. Truthfulness stands as a cornerstone of moral character, requiring steadfastness even in adversity.

Reflection:

How do my natural faculties and moral qualities contribute to my spiritual growth, and am I exercising them at their proper time and place?

How can I discern the proper occasion for exercising qualities like forgiveness and anger, and what role does reason play in balancing these seemingly opposing moral faculties?

Reaction:

Day 31-40: Wake up in the middle of the night and find a quiet, secluded place to sit on the floor in a kneeling position. Read the excerpt and reflect on the questions, supplicating before God for help and guidance. Go back to sleep without engaging in conversation with anyone.

Day 35: Angels

Reading:

Angels play an important role in the spiritual framework. To grasp their correct concept, purpose, and functions, it is essential to explore the nature of angels as creations of God, their relationship with human beings, and their indispensable role as mediators of divine revelation.

Angels are created beings, distinct from humans and other creatures, fashioned by God to fulfill specific roles within the divine order. They are not Divine themselves but are servants of the One True God, endowed with qualities and capacities that enable them to perform their duties faithfully.

In the spiritual realm, angels serve as mediators who facilitate the progress of human beings, much like physical entities in the natural world such as the sun, moon, and clouds bring about essential physical changes. Just as the sun's heat ripens fruits and the winds gather clouds to nourish the earth, angels act as intermediaries conveying divine influence to the hearts of those inclined towards spiritual receptivity. This mediation has been put in place by God because just as physical eyes need light to see, spiritual eyes require the illumination of angels to receive divine revelation and insight. Through their assistance, special individuals who are spiritually prepared can experience profound divine manifestations, enabling their ascent towards nearness to God and spiritual fulfillment. This parallelism between the physical and spiritual world helps us comprehend the unseen forces of nature.

The primary purpose of angels is to carry out the commands of God and to serve as intermediaries between the Divine and the created world. They function continuously to maintain the order and harmony of the universe, both in its visible and invisible aspects.

God has appointed angels as spiritual callers to humanity. Furthermore, angels are involved in the process of revelation: they carry the word of God to the hearts of the recipients of revelation.

While angels are exalted creations, their rank is not necessarily superior to that of humans. Certain perfect human beings, elevated by their spiritual achievements and closeness to God, surpass angels in rank. This elevates humans as the pinnacle of creation, endowed with faculties such as reason, free will, and the capacity for spiritual growth, which angels, though powerful, do not possess in the same way. Angels are created for obedience and service; they do not possess free will in the manner humans do, which makes human spiritual progress and moral responsibility unique.

It is important to understand that God does not need angels or any created beings for His actions but instead He chooses to exercise His power through them to manifest wisdom and to spread knowledge among people. Just like the system of physical means is essential for the development of human understanding and the establishment of sciences such as astronomy, physics, and medicine, similarly, spiritual development follows the same principle, ensuring harmony between the external and internal worlds, the physical and the spiritual.

In summary, angels, as created servants of God, play vital roles in the maintenance of divine order, the execution of divine will, and the mediation of revelation. While they are exalted beings, their rank is not above that of perfected humans, who possess unique faculties and responsibilities. The mediation of angels in revelation mirrors the use of physical means in worldly systems, reflecting God's wisdom in the governance of both seen and unseen worlds. Understanding the true nature and functions of angels enriches the appreciation of divine harmony and the spiritual journey of humankind.

Reflection:

In what ways can I recognize and appreciate the parallels between the physical means through which the natural world operates (e.g., sun, wind) and the spiritual mediation of angels in my own spiritual development?

How does the concept that God chooses to work through created beings, including angels and physical means, affect my understanding of divine wisdom and the balance between external actions and inner spiritual growth?

Reaction:

Day 31-40: Wake up in the middle of the night and find a quiet, secluded place to sit on the floor in a kneeling position. Read the excerpt and reflect on the questions, supplicating before God for help and guidance. Go back to sleep without engaging in conversation with anyone.

Day 36: Revelation

Reading:

Throughout the history of humanity, revelation has played a pivotal role in shaping our understanding of God and His message for humankind. It serves as the celestial bridge between the Divine and the human soul, providing clear guidance about our purpose, the nature of existence, and the path to salvation. Without revelation, human beings would be left to navigate the profound mysteries of life and the hereafter through mere conjecture and imagination, a condition that would inevitably lead to error and confusion.

If there exists an All-Wise God Who wishes that we know Him and live according to His divine laws, it is only reasonable to conclude that He must have established a means to convey His message to humanity. This communication is not incidental; rather, it is a necessary component of the divine plan. Since God created this world as a test for humanity, He must have instituted a system to communicate the rules of this test through His chosen servants. The Law of Nature itself demands this, for God, in His infinite wisdom, has not left mankind to guesswork regarding the purpose of this life, matters of the afterlife, and the ultimate reality of His Being.

The concept of revelation can be likened to a celestial signal from the Divine. Just as a radio receiver must be tuned to the correct frequency and possess the necessary internal components to capture and translate a signal into intelligible sound, so too must the human heart be spiritually purified, aligned with God's will, and endowed with the capacity to receive and comprehend the divine message. This spiritual tuning and purification enables the recipient to perceive the presence of God and His guidance in a manner beyond mere intellectual assent.

This system of revelation is not limited to a particular era but is a continuous process, designed to meet the ongoing spiritual needs of humanity. Even after the full and complete set of divine laws and guidelines having been revealed, human nature remains error-prone and susceptible to faltering. Hence, periodic reinforcement and clarification through continued revelation are essential to keep humanity aligned with the truth. This enduring need for divine guidance underlines the timeless nature of revelation. Those who confine revelation to a specific era deny the infinite grace of God and overlook the fundamental reality that human nature is inherently prone to error.

It must be understood that not everyone is a recipient of revelation. The privilege of receiving frequent divine revelation is reserved for those chosen by God, who have attained a particular level of spiritual purity and sincerity. This selection depends on various factors, including the individual's receptivity, the mercy of God, and the specific needs of the time. Thus, revelation is granted according to divine wisdom and the readiness of the recipient, ensuring that the message is delivered through worthy vessels.

Those who receive this revelation and convey it to humanity are known as prophets. They form the essential link in God's system of guidance, which has been in place since time immemorial. Prophets receive the divine message through revelation, guiding them on the path of righteousness and salvation. Their lives exemplify submission to God's will and serve as living testimonies of the truth of their message.

Therefore, it must be acknowledged that throughout history, there have existed God's chosen people—prophets and messengers—who have been recipients of this divine revelation. These individuals, purified in heart and soul and favored by God's mercy and grace, have acted as conduits for God's message, conveying His commandments and wisdom to the rest of humanity. Their role is indispensable in the divine scheme, as they serve as the mirrors through which God's attributes and laws are reflected to humankind.

A crucial distinction must be made between revelation and thoughts or ideas that arise purely from human effort. Revelation, by its very nature, is a communication from God, free from human invention or speculation. While a chosen servant of God may possess immense knowledge and insight, any concepts emerging solely from their personal reasoning or reflection do not constitute revelation. The fundamental purpose of revelation is to convey God's pure and unadulterated message to humanity, untarnished by human subjectivity or error.

In summary, revelation is the divinely ordained means through which God communicates His will, knowledge, and guidance to humanity. It is a necessary and ongoing process, designed to address the spiritual needs of humankind across all ages. Revelation is distinct from human thought, and reserved for chosen individuals whose purity and sincerity prepare them to receive and transmit God's message at a time and place of God's choosing. Through this sacred channel, prophets have conveyed the laws and wisdom necessary for human salvation, fulfilling God's purpose in creating the world as a test for the hereafter. Recognizing the vital role of revelation enriches our understanding of faith and underscores the profound connection between the Creator and His creation.

Reflection:

How do I understand the necessity of divine revelation in guiding humanity, especially regarding matters beyond human reason and perception?

How do I perceive the role of prophets as recipients of revelation and essential links between God and humanity, and what lessons can I draw from their example in my own spiritual journey?

Reaction:

Day 31-40: Wake up in the middle of the night and find a quiet, secluded place to sit on the floor in a kneeling position. Read the excerpt and reflect on the questions, supplicating before God for help and guidance. Go back to sleep without engaging in conversation with anyone.

Day 37: Death

Reading:

Death is an inevitable reality ordained by God, a decree from which no living being can escape. Regardless of the advancements in science or human ingenuity, death remains a certainty, woven into the fabric of existence by divine will. Our experience since the creation of life affirms that every soul shall taste death at its appointed time, a truth that no amount of human effort can alter.

Throughout history and into the modern age, many have sought to defy death by various means, including the contemporary pursuit of cryogenics and other scientific endeavors aimed at prolonging life indefinitely. However, these attempts are ultimately futile, as death is not merely a biological event but a part of God's absolute law of nature. It is a reality deeply rooted in divine wisdom, beyond the reach of human manipulation or delay.

Death serves as a profound reminder of human limits and helplessness. No matter how wealthy, learned, or powerful one may be, death arrives with certainty, illustrating that life is a trust from God and that we remain creatures dependent on His will. This awareness should inspire humility, prompting individuals to live purposefully and in conscious recognition of their mortality. The certainty of death encourages believers to shed arrogance and self-sufficiency, replacing these with humility and devotion to the True God, the one and only Eternal Being.

The process of death and what follows is beautifully mirrored in the phenomenon of sleep. During sleep, both body and soul enter a temporary state akin to death: the qualities that define wakefulness diminish, consciousness recedes, and the soul undergoes a form of rest. Upon waking, the soul and body are revived, returning to the state of life and awareness. This cycle serves as a living example of the greater transition that death represents. Just as we arise from sleep to consciousness, so too will we be resurrected in the hereafter after our permanent death. This understanding provides comfort and insight to the believer into the nature of existence beyond this temporal world.

Death is not a punishment but a necessary consequence of life under the divine law of nature. It underscores the finiteness of all created beings—animate and inanimate alike. The sun, the moon, animals, plants, and even the smallest particles are mortal and subject to change and cessation. Only God Himself is eternal and unchanging, free from death, destruction, or any deficiency. His attributes are perfect and everlasting, making Him the sole Being worthy of worship and reliance.

Moreover, death reminds us that just as God granted us life out of nothingness, He will cause us to die and subsequently grant us a new life in the hereafter. This transition from the temporal world to the eternal realm is a fundamental tenet of faith and serves as the ultimate purpose and destination for humanity.

In summary, death is a divinely ordained reality that no one can evade. It is a manifestation of God's absolute decree and a necessary part of the natural order. Attempts to circumvent death through human means are bound to fail, as death is the inevitable end of the finite. Recognizing this truth fosters humility, prompts reflection on the purpose of life, and encourages steadfastness in faith. The phenomenon of sleep offers an insightful analogy to understand death and resurrection, reminding us that life and death are interconnected stages in the journey of the soul. Ultimately, death points us to the One True God, the Eternal and Ever-Living, and to the promise of a new life beyond this world. Embracing this understanding leads to a purposeful life dedicated to the worship and love of God.

Reflection:

How does the certainty of death influence my understanding of humility and dependence on God's will in my daily life?

How might recognizing death as a divine decree, rather than a punishment, change the way I approach life's challenges and my spiritual growth?

Reaction:

Day 31-40: Wake up in the middle of the night and find a quiet, secluded place to sit on the floor in a kneeling position. Read the excerpt and reflect on the questions, supplicating before God for help and guidance. Go back to sleep without engaging in conversation with anyone.

Day 38: Hereafter

Reading:

The concept of the hereafter occupies a fundamental position in the edifice of faith. On the surface, it appears as a promise extended to all creation—a life beyond this worldly existence where every individual will be held accountable for their deeds. The righteous will receive reward and joy, while the wrongdoers will face punishment. However, the reality of the hereafter is far more profound and deeply woven into the fabric of reason and divine wisdom.

If the hereafter were merely a promise designed to encourage adherence to moral codes in this life, it would be vulnerable to skepticism and criticism. Like other divine declarations, the hereafter rests on sound reason. Reason alone, however, cannot fully grasp the reality of this eternal life; faith is essential to secure firm conviction in its existence and significance. The human intellect, while powerful, can only travel so far as to recognize the necessity of a Creator and a life beyond this transient world, but certainty about the hereafter emerges through divine revelation and spiritual insight.

Assuming life is confined solely to this world leads to a collapse of even the basic concept of justice. Many in this world live unjustly without facing consequences, while others suffer injustices without redress. If this life were all there is, the perfect justice and mercy of God would remain unmanifested, contradicting the fundamental divine attributes. The hereafter, being more permanent and transcendent, ensures that divine justice, mercy, and grace are fully displayed beyond the veils and limitations of this world.

God's attribute of creation is a testament to the existence of the hereafter. Just as God created life from nothingness, He will resurrect human beings after death to grant them a new life in which they will be called to account for their earthly deeds. This temporary life of the world is a test, designed for humans to exercise their God-given faculties—reason, love, faith, moral choice, etc.—under divine guidance to attain their ultimate purpose.

The hereafter is not solely a distant promise; it can be experienced in this very world through faith and the love of God. A true believer perceives signs of the hereafter, such as peace, contentment, and spiritual delight, which strengthen their certainty in the life to come. The interplay of faith, righteous action, and divine grace creates an inner paradise, while neglect and sin generate spiritual torment, both manifesting here and now as precursors of what awaits beyond.

True salvation involves liberation from the hell of sin in this life, beginning with the certainty of faith and an intimate recognition of God. Belief in the hereafter motivates one to avoid sin, not merely out of fear of punishment, but from love, reverence, and a deep understanding of divine justice. This transformative faith helps believers tread the path of righteousness and spiritual growth.

Ultimately, the purpose of life culminates in the return to the Creator with a heart and soul at peace, firm in faith and conviction. This tranquility at the time of death is the fruit of a life lived in awareness of the hereafter, sustained by prayer, repentance, steadfastness, and love for God. The believer's journey is thus marked not only by hope in the hereafter but by the experience of its blessings in this world.

In summary, the hereafter is a cornerstone of faith, deeply intertwined with reason, divine justice, and spiritual experience. It transcends a mere promise of future reward or punishment and is foundational for understanding the purpose of life and the manifestation of divine attributes. While reason points towards its necessity, faith illuminates its reality, allowing believers to experience signs of the hereafter in this life. Justice, mercy, and grace find their full expression in the hereafter, where every soul is recompensed according to its deeds. Prayer, repentance, and steadfastness are vital means to prepare for and partake in the hereafter. Ultimately, the believer's goal is to return to God with soul at peace, having attained both spiritual fulfillment in this life and success in the next.

Reflection:

How does my understanding of the hereafter influence my perception of justice and mercy in this world, especially in situations where injustice seems to prevail?

How do I currently experience signs of the hereafter—such as peace, contentment, or spiritual delight—in my life, and what practices (prayer, repentance, steadfastness) can strengthen this inner realization?

Reflecting on the purpose of life as a test and preparation for the hereafter, how am I aligning my heart and soul towards returning to God with tranquility and firm faith?

Reaction:

Day 31-40: Wake up in the middle of the night and find a quiet, secluded place to sit on the floor in a kneeling position. Read the excerpt and reflect on the questions, supplicating before God for help and guidance. Go back to sleep without engaging in conversation with anyone.

Day 39: Religion

Reading:

A vast diversity of religions exist in the world today and an exploration of their individual doctrines is beyond our current scope. What we would rather focus on is the more fundamental question regarding the need for religion: If the All-Wise God has chosen that His creation should worship Him and live harmoniously, would He not have provided guidance on how to achieve this purpose? To suppose otherwise would be to attribute a lack of wisdom to God, which is inconceivable.

As we observe human development throughout history, we see a clear evolutionary progression in physical, mental, and spiritual capacities. Just as a child begins with basic knowledge and gradually ascends to more complex subjects in education, so too must divine guidance evolve with humanity's readiness. The system of guidance that God provided in the form of religious teachings must not have been a static, one-size-fits-all revelation but an unfolding process tailored to human capacities over time. This evolutionary approach ensured that humanity throughout history was not overwhelmed by concepts beyond its developmental stage but was instead nurtured gradually towards spiritual maturity.

At its core, religion is the divine mechanism by which humans acquire certainty of faith in God's existence and attributes. This certainty is not mere intellectual assent but a profound recognition that transforms the individual, leading to deliverance from sin and the blossoming of true love of God and His creation. Religion thus guides humans to obtain mastery over their passions and develop a personal love for God, which is described as spiritual heaven manifesting in diverse forms in the hereafter. Conversely, ignorance of the True God, estrangement from Him, and absence of love for Him result in spiritual hell.

Religion must not merely be a set of rituals or disputes but a comprehensive, perfect system that is free from defects in its doctrines, commandments, and teachings. It must stand the test of reason and provide living blessings that manifest in this world, offering evidence of its divine origin and truth. Faith grounded in reason but complemented by revelation and spiritual insight is the pathway to true understanding.

A common criticism of religion is that it has been a source of conflict and division. However, this view overlooks the essence of true religion. Genuine religion seeks not to sow discord but to cultivate righteousness, peace, and harmony among people. Disputes and harsh words conducted in the name of religion are not reflective of religion itself but of human failings and misunderstandings.

Another prevalent misconception arises from the fantastical stories and myths often attributed to religious traditions and their holy figures. Such tales, if taken as the foundation of faith, reduce religion to superstition and idolatry. True religion, however, is founded on reason and rational inquiry, even though reason alone cannot establish firm belief. A vital element of faith complements reason, where faith is not blind but grounded on rational foundations and supported by divine revelation.

Since religion is the guidance from the Creator to His creation, it follows that this guidance must be conveyed through a deliberate and divinely appointed process. God, in His infinite wisdom, has chosen to communicate His will through revelation, transmitted through angels to prophets. These prophets, in turn, convey the divine message to humanity. The codification of these revelations forms the body of religion, which serves as the essential guide for humankind to achieve the ultimate purpose of life: understanding God, establishing a relationship with Him through worship, and living peacefully with others.

This process is beautifully designed to align with human capacities and spiritual needs. Just as physical needs are met through a system of natural laws and mediators (like the sun's heat ripening fruits or winds assembling clouds), spiritual needs are met through the system of revelation and spiritual intermediaries. The angels, as God's agents, facilitate the communication of divine knowledge and blessings, ensuring a harmonious balance between the physical and spiritual realms. The prophets, being human themselves, serve as models of perfect human beings who exemplify the teachings of God in their lives.

In summary, religion is the divinely ordained system of guidance that evolved alongside human capacities, designed to lead humankind towards the ultimate goal of life: a deep understanding and loving relationship with the One True God. It transcends superstition and blind faith by being grounded in reason and supported by faith. Religion manifests as a comprehensive, perfect system of guidance that offers deliverance from sin and fosters true love and fear of God. The mechanism of revelation, angels, and prophets is the comprehensive means through which God communicates His will to humanity. Far from being a source of conflict, true religion is the pathway to peace, righteousness, and spiritual fulfillment, guiding humankind towards salvation in this life and the hereafter.

Reflection:

How can I distinguish between the true essence of religion as a source of guidance and peace, and the human errors or misunderstandings that cause conflict and division in its name?

Am I open to the concept of evolution in regards to the development of world religions?

Reaction:

Day 31-40: Wake up in the middle of the night and find a quiet, secluded place to sit on the floor in a kneeling position. Read the excerpt and reflect on the questions, supplicating before God for help and guidance. Go back to sleep without engaging in conversation with anyone.

Day 40: Prophets

Reading:

Prophets hold a unique and exalted status among the holy personages in the grand scheme of creation. Their role is exclusive and pivotal—they serve as the vital link between God and humanity, entrusted with conveying the divine message to humankind. This connection is fundamental because God, while being the ultimate source of guidance, chooses to communicate His will and wisdom through these specially appointed human beings, who exemplify the teachings they deliver.

The decision regarding when and upon whom prophethood is bestowed lies solely with God. This divine prerogative is not arbitrary but is based on the capacity and ability of the individual combined with the spiritual and temporal needs of the age. Prophets appear in times when the world is engulfed in spiritual darkness and moral decay, emerging as reformers who restore the light of true guidance. Their advent is a manifestation of God's mercy and grace, sent to awaken humanity from heedlessness and guide them toward righteousness.

Although prophets are exalted figures, they remain human beings. Throughout history, followers of various prophets have often exaggerated their nature, attributing to them supernatural status beyond what is warranted. In reality, prophets are distinguished by their nearness to God and their divinely commissioned purpose. Their humanity is essential to their role as models for humankind; they walk the same earthly path with the same human faculties, making their guidance accessible and relevant to all.

God's infinite wisdom is evident in His choice to utilize human messengers for conveying divine guidance rather than angels or other superhumans. If guidance had been given solely by angels, human beings could have excused themselves from following it, claiming incapacity to emulate such beings. Prophets, being human, live out the teachings practically and perfectly, showing humanity how to apply divine guidance in daily life. This embodiment of divine principles removes any excuse for neglecting or rejecting the path of righteousness.

God is independent and free from all needs; He does not require worship or obedience. Rather, He sends prophets out of sheer grace and mercy, providing humanity with the means to attain spiritual salvation and peace. Despite this, history reveals that prophets often endure trials, tribulations, and rejection by the very people they are sent to guide. They are met with hostility simply because they call people back to belief in the One True God. Yet, despite persecution, prophets remain beacons of love, forgiveness, and mercy, reflecting God's boundless compassion for humankind.

The truth of a prophet's claim is evidenced by both his life before and after the proclamation of prophethood. A truthful and upright life prior to the claim establishes credibility, as it demonstrates the moral and spiritual integrity necessary for such a divine mission. Following this, the successful completion of the prophetic mission, often against enormous odds, serves as proof of divine help and support. If a claimant were false, God would not grant success in fulfilling the mission. Thus, the authenticity of a prophet's life and mission collectively testify to the truth of his divine appointment.

Prophets are not mere optional figures but indispensable components of the divine system of religious guidance. Acceptance of their message is a necessary condition for true belief in God. The recognition of a prophet and adherence to his teachings underpin faith and salvation. They are mirrors reflecting the countenance of God, and through them, believers see and understand the Divine more clearly.

In summary, prophets occupy a singular and vital position in the relationship between God and humanity. God alone determines the timing and recipients of prophethood, raising these chosen individuals to guide humankind in times of spiritual darkness. While prophets are humans, their lives exemplify perfect submission and closeness to God, making divine guidance tangible and attainable. Their mission is a manifestation of divine grace, and despite facing rejection and hardship, they embody love, mercy, and forgiveness. The truth of their prophethood is substantiated by their lives and the divine success they achieve. Ultimately, prophets are essential to the system of divine guidance, and belief in them is inseparable from belief in God.

Reflection:

How does understanding the humanity of prophets affect the way I relate to their teachings and example in my daily life?

How do the trials and hardships faced by prophets inspire me to remain steadfast in my own faith and commitment to righteousness?

Reaction:

Day 31-40: Wake up in the middle of the night and find a quiet, secluded place to sit on the floor in a kneeling position. Read the excerpt and reflect on the questions, supplicating before God for help and guidance. Go back to sleep without engaging in conversation with anyone.

Conclusion

In a world plagued with distractions, it is easy to overlook the most profound proof of the existence of God: the miracle of existence itself. Take the hypothetical experience of waking up each morning to find a perfectly made breakfast on the table—one crafted to your needs and requirements. You've never seen the person who prepares the breakfast or lays out the table perfectly for your use but without fail, day after day, it's there for you with conscious design and purposeful intent. You would be deemed insane to claim that the breakfast gets created day after day by chance and there is no one preparing it simply because you haven't "seen" them.

This crude analogy helps illustrate the state of affairs for those who refuse to accept the existence of a Divine Being Who has laid out this world with conscious design and purposeful intent for the benefit of humankind. Day after day, we continue to benefit from the sun, moon, water, vegetation, animals, and countless other things at the micro and macroscopic level that are perfectly created and sustained for our benefit. Yet, will we continue to persist that this universe was created—and continues to be sustained—as a result of some random chance?

The above is a theoretical argument for the existence of God and one that has been debated by philosophers and scientists for centuries. What we present in this book is an approach that addresses both the theory and experiment.

We know from the scientific method that a theory needs experimental verification in order to be accepted as truth. But unless the theory is correct, no amount of experimentation will result in confirming its truth. Therefore, we dedicated the first part of this book to describing the true concept of God—the correct theory. Only then could we be adequately prepared to carry out the subsequent step of verifying it through experience.

Belief in God has to be based on true knowledge of Him. Without correct knowledge, belief is subject to being shaken. For example, if your concept of God consists of deifying a human being or an animal, no matter how strong your belief or experience may be, it will never be effective because it is fundamentally false. And falsehood can never be converted into truth no matter how many people believe it or how strongly they believe it. This is because truth cannot be made up; rather it is supported by nature, which itself is established by the source of all truth—God Himself.

But theory itself is not sufficient. Having the correct theory about God that is based on truth only gets one to the stage of God *should* exist—that is, the probability of God existing is higher than the probability of God not existing. In order to go from God *should* exist to the stage of God *does* exist, one must experience God—that is, confirm the theory with experiment. And this is the purpose behind the second part of the book: to take the reader, who has established themselves on true and firm footing that God should exist, through the stages where they experience God themselves, resulting in the strong conviction that God does exist. This approach is conclusively superior to the intellectual or theoretical approach that many philosophers and scientists of the past indulged in for centuries because it uses both the mind and the heart to arrive at the truth.

What the philosophers and scientists failed to realize in their pursuit of answering the question of God's existence was that He is not something to be seen with the physical eye or to be heard by the sensory ear or even to be understood by the intellectual brain. That approach would be akin to saying that love doesn't exist because you can't see it. For someone who experiences love, it can be the strongest of feelings. People throughout history have given up their lives in pursuit of the beloved. What was it that drove them to forgo their very existence over a feeling that they couldn't see or touch or even comprehend? It was the power of experience. Once they experienced love, they did not need to see love, they did not need to touch love, and they did not need any arguments to understand love. No matter what rationale people may have given them against the reality of love, it amounted to nothing when compared to the experience of love.

Similarly, if you try to convince someone that they should put their hand in fire and it won't burn because fire is simply a combination of fuel and oxygen, they would never do it. No amount of scientific proof will convince them to take this suicidal step. Why? Because they have experience that speaks to the contrary. And experience leads to the strongest form of belief.

While these examples help to illustrate the point, they are crude when compared to experiencing True God. The point however remains that God is not to be seen with the physical eye or heard through the physical ear or touched by the physical hand. God is to be experienced by the heart and soul of a believer. Insisting that God doesn't exist because we can't see him through the physical eye or hear him through the physical ear is akin to demanding that we be able to see the fragrance of a rose or hear the deliciousness of a well-cooked meal. This would be deemed nothing short of madness. Ultimately, the right sense must be used for the right purpose. It is the height of tragic irony that the God Who gave us the means to comprehend the physical world through our eyes, ears, hands, nose, and tongue also gave us the mind through which to attempt to understand Him and the heart through which to attempt to experience His Being. But we insist on relegating our understanding and experience of God to the physical senses. He is not of this world and thus the senses of this world cannot discover Him. Our heart is the vessel for God. But it requires that this vessel be cleansed of all arrogance and pride. And once you experience God, no amount of logic or science or philosophy can deter you against it. In fact you start to view such logical, scientific or philosophical arguments with a sense of pity because you know that your conviction is based upon something that the logicians, scientists and philosophers simply don't have—the experience of True God.

Again, both the mind and the heart need to be convinced that the God we believe in is indeed the One True God. Otherwise, faith devoid of reason is unfounded and mere fantasy. And reason without faith is shallow and mere philosophy.

One of the arguments made in this book is that once we understand the true concept of God and experience Him, then the question whether God exists or not becomes irrelevant. Arguments are inferior to well-grounded experience when it comes to proving the existence of something. In other words, experience is the most advanced stage of belief and no arguments remain necessary to prove the existence of something once we have experienced it.

But like anything else in life that is worth achieving, recognizing True God requires sincere and persistent effort. Athletes spend all their lives just to be able to attain the highest level in their sport. Scholars spend a lifetime focused on solving a problem or making a discovery. So why must we give up so quickly on our pursuit of God, the Creator and Sustainer of everything that we see around us? It stands to reason that the search for God must be done with the highest of persistence, more than any worldly pursuit. And this recognition is not meant to be a brief experiment or a passing phase, but a lifelong transformation. To discover True God and then return to the old status quo would be like finding the greatest treasure only to abandon it.

As human beings, we must understand our status and responsibility in the ecosystem of creation. Human beings stand as the pinnacle of all living species in this world. There is no other creation in the world that stands superior in terms of mental and spiritual capabilities when compared with the human species. Not only are we endowed with superior intellectual and spiritual capacities, human beings have been granted a distinct quality that makes us particularly suitable for collective progressive evolution: we are able to transfer our knowledge across generations using an advanced form of communication (i.e. language). This is not true with other creations. For example, an ox continues to perform the same function of tilling the earth today as it did a thousand years ago. The sun serves the purpose of providing heat as it did in the past and will continue to do so in the future. But humanity has progressed in its collective knowledge and continues to do so. This leads to the conclusion that human beings must have a higher purpose in life than to simply be relegated to the pursuit of worldly affairs. Unfortunately, while this quality has allowed humanity to create a civilization that no other creation could do, it has come at a cost: we have chosen to ignore, or in many cases completely deny, the Creator that bestowed this quality upon us in the first place. The reason has to do with the misuse of a God-given faculty that we have been bestowed with: free will.

We've discussed free will already but suffice it to say that it is part and parcel of human nature. God created human beings with the ability to make decisions at an intelligent level and thus be accountable for those decisions. How we use this ability is up to us. Free will is indeed an invaluable trait and one that makes human beings the pinnacle of creation. If God wanted, He could have created a human species devoid of free will but then it would not be considered the pinnacle of creation.

Unfortunately, over the course of time and with the advances in "knowledge", a vast percentage of humanity chose to use this God given ability of free will to deny the very existence of God Who bestowed it on us in the first place. This is the greatest tragic irony of the human race. The cause of this denial has to do with arrogance, a vice that develops in humans as a result of the misuse of God-given faculties.

The history of organized religion is beyond the scope of this book, but it can be shown that arrogance is the root of disobedience to the dictates of God. And any form of progress, be it physical, mental, or even spiritual, if left unchecked, gets tarnished by arrogance. For example, when a student sets out to acquire knowledge and is successful to some degree, this success can come at the cost of a feeling of superiority, causing the student to fall prey to arrogance and think that he knows more than others. This can have detrimental effects in that instead of acquiring knowledge, the student would deviate away from this goal and go down a path that runs counter to it. In this day and age, humanity has collectively fallen victim to arrogance and has come to a conclusion that we as human beings know more than God—this is effectively what we are saying when we deny the existence of God. As we stated earlier, this is particularly tragic given that God is the One Who gave us the means to acquire and develop knowledge in the first place.

But rest assured. God has given human beings the remedy for this illness as well. And it is none other than the faculty we identified at the outset as one that was necessary for us to embrace while taking on this journey in search of True God: humility.

Humility is a faculty of human beings and is the elixir to the illness that is arrogance. It is only through cultivating humility that one can counter the ill effects of arrogance. To help understand the importance of humility, we can take the same example of a student who sets out on the path of acquiring knowledge—this time with a feeling of humility. Such a student is much more likely to attain success in his endeavors because true and sincere humility demands that one does not fall prey to arrogance and maintains focus on the intended goal. Therefore, humility is a basic requirement for success. And if we see this phenomenon being applicable in the acquisition of worldly knowledge, how is it possible that it wouldn't apply in the case of the infinite source of all knowledge, God Himself? The fact is that humility is absolutely necessary if we hope to understand and build a relationship with the True God.

In summary, God created us with two key components with which to recognize and develop a relationship with our Creator: the mind—to understand Him—and the heart—to experience Him. Further, as the pinnacle of His creation, He endowed us with a complete and fully developed form of free will, a great blessing that is exclusive to human beings. Yet, with the passage of time and with the acquisition of "knowledge", we let our arrogance take the best of us, gradually overtaking any feelings of humility we may have possessed, resulting in complete denial of God altogether. But there is hope. We can take this journey of understanding and experiencing God with humility and dedication. We can choose to undo this tragedy by embracing God, one soul at a time. Free will, the same faculty that may have caused the tragic denial of God, can allow us to embrace Him if wrapped in the mantle of humility, commitment, and open-mindedness. It is up to each one of us. This is such an important endeavor—both at an individual and at the societal level—that our very survival depends on it.

This may, at first glance, seem like an exaggerated claim but taking a step back and observing the state of the world throughout history should help us better understand the issue. As mentioned earlier, human beings represent the pinnacle of creation as a result of their unique God-given capabilities. But these capabilities, if misused and abused by human beings themselves, can result in them sinking to the lowest depths of vice and sin. History is replete with tragic examples of individuals and nations in power committing the most heinous acts, perpetuating cycles of evil that at times seem unending. Such evil groups have always been small in number, yet wield immense power, and rely on disunity of the masses to carry out their objectives. Understood in this light, it is truly a battle between good and evil: good—by virtue of the pure natural faculties bestowed upon us by God at birth—is vast in number and inherent in all human beings, while evil—arising from a small group of individuals' abuse and misuse of these natural faculties—is few in number yet becomes a dominating and controlling force. In order to carry out their plans, these evil but powerful people rely on disunity that they sow amongst the good-natured masses. Thus, the only effective way to defeat this powerful evil is through unity. But unity formed under any man-made banner—whether national, racial, or ideological, no matter how noble or well-intentioned—cannot produce true universal unity. Only by uniting under the banner of One True God, transcending artificial barriers of color, ethnicity, or politics, can we hope to see good overcome evil.

God, being the Master of everything, has ordained that goodness will ultimately prevail over evil, but this victory is contingent upon following *His* divine plan and our collective unification under *His* banner. It is also important to understand that this divine plan is not limited to our existence; it is a cross-generational plan that will take time to manifest. This realization puts an added responsibility upon us to not just recognize True God and live our lives according to His wishes but also to inculcate the same realization in our surroundings, starting with our own progeny. It is with this conviction that we must live and spread the message of True God—not for any worldly sake or ambition but because the sanctity and gravity of the task itself demands it and the survival of the human race depends upon it.

Once we understand that our survival is dependent on recognizing True God and following His plan, the question of how hard or easy that task is becomes irrelevant. After all, when we are faced with a life-threatening situation, we don't sit there postulating whether we should or should not take the necessary steps to save our life—we do whatever is necessary to pursue the path to survival no matter how difficult it may be. But for the sake of argument, we will address the topic of the difficulty of pursuing the path towards God.

Some may think that living by the dictates of God is too difficult or overly constraining. This is a misplaced opinion. The fact is that if the totality of human existence consists of mind, body, and soul, then it stands to reason that the full human experience must be one that caters to the needs of all three components. If we were to live a life solely focused on fulfilling the desires of the body, it would not be considered a "full life". We see many examples of this in stories of individuals who spent their youth involved in shallow, temporary relationships only to be left with a great sense of regret and loss in their advanced age at not attaining a lasting, meaningful relationship based on true love. Likewise, someone who spends their life engrossed in books for the development of the mind to the point of sacrificing their bodily well-being would be left with all sorts of health issues. God is our Creator and has infused us with certain needs for the mind, body and soul. He is best positioned to identify how to fulfill those needs while keeping in mind the ultimate objective of human creation. It stands to reason that the perfect set of rules and regulations, as defined by God Himself, could not have ignored these needs. Instead, rather than leaving us to fulfill these needs impulsively like animals, living in accordance with the dictates of God provides a refined path for doing so. So the optimal human experience is to live a balanced life that addresses the needs of the mind, body, and soul keeping in mind the divine rules and regulations. And doing so does not prevent one from enjoying the bounties of life; rather it encourages a fine balance amongst the bounties spanning across the three components of human existence. This in turn results in a more refined, sophisticated, and enjoyable life experience, regulated by rules that are created for the betterment of humanity, which, in essence, is what differentiates us from animals.

The question then arises: who is best suited to come up with these rules and regulations that would dictate human affairs? In a godless society, these rules have to be left to human beings to come up with (since there is no concept of a Higher Power in such a society). There are many problems with this approach. First, who amongst human beings would be considered suitable to define these rules and regulations against which all of the rest of humanity is to abide by? If one group decides to take up the mantle, the others would have a right to object. If we say that the intellectually superior humans would naturally rise to this position and therefore be the ones to take on this privilege, we quickly see the flaw with this approach as well since human beings suffer from multiple weaknesses—greed, arrogance, selfish hunger for power to name a few. History, as evidenced by abuse of power by rulers across many empires, is a testament to this fact. A typical follow-on argument may be made that we could democratically elect members from amongst a group and entrust them with developing the regulations. But again, this approach suffers from flaws as well. While the democratically elected process could be considered suitable for the implementation of the regulations, the fact remains that selecting human beings to *define* the actual rules and regulations that apply to humans themselves is a fundamentally flawed approach. The reason comes back to the premise that human beings are error prone—they suffer from weaknesses, lack of knowledge and foresight, limitations in capabilities, ulterior motives, etc. Therefore, they cannot produce a perfect set of rules and regulations for themselves. So any man-made system of rules and regulations—be it capitalism, socialism, or communism to name a few—is bound to fail. We soon come to the realization that while we as human beings can carry out the implementation of these rules and regulations (since they are for our operation and progress), we are certainly not qualified to define such rules. Only a Superior Being is qualified to carry out this undertaking—the One Who created us and knows what is best for us. And this applies at all levels, from regulations on how to live one individual life all the way to regulations that allow us to best live with each other on an international scale.

This analysis leads us to the following conclusion: *Belief in and practice of the teachings (rules and regulations) of God is essential at every level of our existence.* Individual peace and satisfaction cannot be attained without belief in God. Family peace and harmony cannot be achieved without belief in God. Social and international peace requires belief in God and following the rules and regulations laid out by Him for peaceful coexistence.

The basic phenomenon of life (as it is created and sustained) is a result of the two attributes of God—Creator and Sustainer. And if, as we have shown, the very basic and foundational purpose of this world is to allow for life to continue existing, then it stands to reason that the One Who created and sustains life must necessarily have provided a code or a set of guidelines not just for this to occur, but do so in the best manner. This code or set of guidelines must exist for all creation, including plants, animals, and of course, the pinnacle of creation—human beings. In the case of non-human life, this code is not necessarily documented in a verbal or written form but rather in the form of "laws of nature". For example, plants need water and sunlight in order to survive—this is part of the code for plant life. Some animals eat plants and vegetation in order to survive while others prey on fellow animals to sustain life. This is the code for animal life. Even at the level of microorganisms, we find processes for the continuation of life. For example, bacteria needs a certain type of environment in order to survive, without which it ceases to exist. This again is the code for life of microorganisms.

When it comes to human beings, a similar "law of nature" has been instituted by God, but in a much more advanced and sophisticated form. Since human life is intelligent—that is, human beings have been endowed with a faculty to communicate at an advanced level—the code or set of guidelines given by God as it relates to human beings takes a more advanced shape in the form of a verbal or written code or set of guidelines. We can simply refer to this code or set of guidelines for human beings as "religion". Viewed in this light, religion is a necessary part of human life for it provides human beings with a code or set of guidelines that, at the most basic level, allow life to exist and, at the most advanced level, allow the inhabitants to build the optimal relationship with their Creator and with each other. Given that there is an All-Wise God Who created us and sustains us, it stands to reason that He must have revealed a code for us to live by. Otherwise, the mere act of creation without a code or set of guidelines to sustain it, would not be considered wise. Therefore, we conclude that an All-Wise God must necessarily have revealed the perfect religion.

The fact is that there *is* a God but we as a society have chosen to deny His existence. And this denial has left a collective void within us that cannot be filled with anything else. The God that created us also created this special space in our hearts that can only be occupied by His remembrance. But again, as part and parcel of free will, He gave us the freedom to do so, or deny it and face the destructive consequences. The current day unrest—from personal disorders to international conflicts—testifies to this fact. Cases of drug abuse and suicide amongst the youth, unspeakable crimes committed in society, normalization of gender dysphoria, declining birth rates, endless wars, and exploitation of resources by the haves against the have nots are just few examples.

The solution to all these problems is to embrace the fact that there is a True God Who is more powerful and loving than the "collective us" and He expects us to live by the rules and guidelines He has laid out for us for our own benefit. At the very basic stage, this conviction instills in us a fear of the power of God and impels us to avoid evil. And as we progress on this journey to more advanced stages, it cultivates a love for God, motivating us to do good. It is this combination of fear and love of God that will lead us to attain peace at all levels by following His rules and guidance. It is incumbent upon us to investigate and identify this set of rules and guidance—which we hereby define as True Religion—and that is a subject for another book.

If this book helped improve your understanding of God, please consider leaving a brief review on Amazon or Goodreads. Your words might be exactly what someone else needs to hear as they begin their own journey toward recognizing and building a relationship with True God.

For related content, please visit the author's website:

fmpal.net

www.ingramcontent.com/pod-product-compliance
Lightning Source LLC
LaVergne TN
LVHW010652110826
845149LV00014B/3047
9781972377000